FAKING IT

how to cook delicious food without really trying

delicious.

For Phil, Toby and Henry, who have been with me through
every breakfast, lunch and dinner (the good, the bad and
the ugly) and never complained... I love you all.

delicious.
FAKING IT

how to cook delicious food without really trying

VALLI LITTLE

Photography by Brett Stevens

HarperCollins*PublishersLtd*

CONTENTS

LE CHEF !
A TOUJOURS
RAISON

Welcome to my world... It's a pretty hectic one where, like most of you, I spend a great deal of time juggling all the elements that make life fulfilling and fun – home and work, family and friends.

Although cooking is my passion, finding time for it isn't always easy. I think the idea for this book first came to me one evening while I was on the phone to a publisher, clearing the debris our new puppy had created around the house, and running late to pick up my son from rugby training. Oh, and I was trying to wrap a beef fillet in pastry, as we were having friends around for dinner.

So I started thinking about ways to make the kind of food I love, but keep it simple. Don't get me wrong – 'faking it' doesn't mean you can't stay true to the way you like to cook and entertain, it's just about taking a few clever shortcuts.

Delis, gourmet food shops and many supermarkets stock an ever-increasing range of helpful items, such as quality pasta sauces, curry pastes and roasted or chargrilled vegetables. Together with a little planning and a few fresh ingredients, these products make it easy to create impressive dishes.

These days, I save restaurant-style, four-course dinners for when I go out. When cooking for family or friends at home, I opt for delicious, easy-to-prepare dinners that still call in the compliments.

My food is the product of many influences. My childhood in England encouraged my love of fresh, seasonal produce (nothing could compare with Dad's first crop of Jersey Royal potatoes or summer raspberries). Then there was the explosion of Thai flavours when I first tasted a betel leaf at Sydney's Longrain. And I always gather inspiration on my travels, whether it's a simple lemon pasta in Italy or an exquisite degustation at Joël Robuchon in Paris.

The recipes in this book reflect all those experiences, and the wonderful chefs and cooks I've worked with for *delicious.* magazine. I wanted to share dishes suited to our busy lives, but which keep the element of fun and excitement that we should all get from cooking.

Turning a few ingredients into a beautiful meal doesn't have to be difficult, but it is an act of love. So there's nothing wrong with using a few shortcuts and *Faking It* sometimes, as long as you always cook with passion!

Valli

vodka salmon with mini rosti

Serves 4 (makes 8-12 rosti)

This is great as a weekend brunch dish served with iced vodka, but works just as well as a midweek dinner.

3 desiree or pontiac potatoes (600g total), peeled
200g smoked salmon slices
2 tbs vodka
2 tbs finely chopped dill, plus sprigs to garnish
2 tsp wholegrain mustard
1/2 cup (120g) creme fraiche or sour cream
2 eggs, beaten
2 tbs rice flour
2 tbs olive oil
Lemon wedges, to serve

Simmer the potatoes in a pan of boiling water for 10 minutes to par-cook. Drain and chill for 30 minutes.

Place the smoked salmon in a shallow dish. Combine the vodka with 1 tablespoon of the chopped dill, then pour over the salmon. Cover and refrigerate until ready to serve.

Combine the mustard and creme fraiche with the remaining chopped dill in a bowl. Refrigerate until needed.

Coarsely grate the cooled potatoes into a bowl. Stir in the egg and rice flour, then season and stir to combine.

Heat the oil in a non-stick frypan over medium heat. Working in batches of 3-4 rosti, add 1 tablespoon of the mixture to the pan for each rosti and flatten slightly. Cook for 2 minutes each side until crisp and brown, then remove and keep warm in a low oven while you cook the remaining rosti.

Place 2-3 rosti on each plate, top with salmon and drizzle with the creme fraiche mixture. Garnish with extra dill sprigs and serve with lemon wedges.

breakfast cranachan

Serves 4

Cranachan is a Scottish dessert made with oats, whisky, berries and honey. It's a great breakfast, too, with or without the whisky.

300g thick Greek-style yoghurt
150ml evaporated milk
Finely grated zest and juice of 1 lemon
250g fresh or frozen (thawed) mixed berries
2 tbs honey, plus extra to drizzle
2 tbs whisky (optional)
3/4 cup (95g) toasted muesli

Place the yoghurt, evaporated milk, lemon zest and juice in a bowl and gently whisk to combine.

In a separate bowl, lightly crush the berries with a fork. Stir in the honey and whisky, if using.

When ready to serve, spoon alternating layers of fruit, muesli and yoghurt into 4 tall glasses. Serve drizzled with extra honey.

toffee-apple pancakes

Serves 4

20g unsalted butter
3 small Granny Smith apples, peeled,
   cored, cut into 2cm pieces
½ firmly packed cup (100g) brown sugar
¼ cup (60ml) Calvados* or brandy
½ cup (125ml) thickened cream, plus extra to serve
400g packet frozen French-style crepes* (8 crepes total)
Icing sugar, to dust

Melt the butter in a frypan over medium heat. Add apple and brown sugar and cook, stirring occasionally, for 5-6 minutes until the sugar dissolves and apple softens slightly. Stir in the Calvados and cream. Cook, stirring occasionally, for 1-2 minutes until the sauce has thickened and the apple is tender.

Meanwhile, warm the crepes according to packet instructions.

Arrange 2 crepes on each serving plate, then spoon over the apples and toffee sauce. Drizzle with extra cream, then serve dusted with icing sugar.

* Calvados is an apple brandy from selected bottle shops. Frozen crepes are available from selected supermarkets (see Glossary).

"round the house" breakfast slice

Serves 4

My husband, Phil, was a Qantas flight steward when we met.
One of the highlights of his London trips was breakfast
at The Mayfair hotel, where they served "round the house"
– a cooked breakfast that included absolutely everything.
This is our homestyle version.

2 tbs olive oil
1 onion, thinly sliced
4 bacon rashers, cut into batons
150g button mushrooms, sliced
500g parboiled or precooked chat potatoes*, quartered
8 cherry tomatoes, halved
1 tbs chopped flat-leaf parsley
8 eggs, beaten
¼ cup (60ml) pure (thin) cream
Tomato sauce (ketchup), to serve

Preheat the oven to 190ºC. Grease a 1.25-litre baking dish.
    Heat the oil in a large frypan over medium heat. Add the
onion and bacon and cook, stirring occasionally, for 2-3 minutes
until onion softens and bacon starts to crisp. Add the mushroom
and potato and cook, stirring occasionally, for 2 minutes or
until the mushroom starts to soften.
    Tip the mixture into the baking dish, then scatter over the
tomatoes and parsley. Beat the eggs and cream together,
season with sea salt and freshly ground black pepper, then
pour into the dish. Bake for 15 minutes or until the egg has
set, then slice and serve with tomato sauce.
* Precooked potatoes are available from selected supermarkets.

summer fruit salad with pikelets

Serves 4

In a perfect world, we'd make our own pikelets, but this is a great way to turn ready-made ones into something special.

2 oranges
2 mangoes
2 bananas, peeled, sliced
250g punnet strawberries, hulled, quartered
1 tbs shredded mint leaves
2 x 200g packets pikelets
Honey or maple syrup, to serve
Icing sugar (optional), to dust

Zest both oranges using a zester, then place the zest in a large bowl. Remove the pith from 1 orange and segment the flesh into the bowl. Thinly slice the flesh of 1 mango and add to the bowl with the banana, strawberries and mint.

Juice the remaining orange, chop the flesh of the remaining mango, then puree both in a blender until smooth. Stir half the puree into the salad, reserving the rest to serve.

Heat the pikelets according to packet instructions, then divide among serving plates. Drizzle with honey or syrup, dust with icing sugar, and serve with the fruit salad and remaining mango puree to drizzle.

"espresso" scrambled eggs

Serves 1-2

Renowned New Zealand caterer Ruth Pretty told me about this clever recipe when I visited her beautiful home and cooking school just outside Wellington. Australia is such a coffee-loving society that many of us own an espresso machine, and now it has a second use. A Bloody Mary makes it extra special.

2 free-range eggs
2 tbs pure (thin) cream
1 tbs finely chopped chives or flat-leaf parsley,
   plus extra to serve
20g unsalted butter, softened
Hot buttered toast, to serve

Place the eggs and cream in the milk-frothing jug of an espresso machine and beat with a fork to combine. Season, then stir in the chives or parsley and butter.

Heat the espresso machine's steam jet according to instructions. Give the espresso machine's steam jet a blast, then place the jug under the jet and cook the egg mixture, swirling the jug, for 2-3 minutes until the eggs are just set (the mixture should be soft and light). Serve the scrambled eggs on hot buttered toast, garnished with extra chives.

deep-fried eggs with asparagus

Serves 4

6 free-range eggs
2 tbs plain flour
1 cup panko breadcrumbs*
Sunflower oil, to deep-fry
2-3 bunches thin asparagus, woody ends trimmed,
   blanched for 3 minutes until tender
2 tbs extra virgin olive oil
1 tbs balsamic vinegar

Place 4 eggs in a pan of cold water, bring to the boil, then cook for 3 minutes to soft-boil. Remove from heat and plunge the eggs into a bowl of iced water.

Beat remaining 2 eggs in a bowl. Place flour and breadcrumbs in 2 separate bowls. Peel the soft-boiled eggs very carefully and gently pat dry with paper towel. Roll the eggs first in the flour, then in the beaten egg and then in the breadcrumbs. Set aside.

Half-fill a deep-fryer or large heavy-based saucepan with sunflower oil and heat to 190°C. (If you don't have a deep-fryer thermometer, test a cube of bread – it will turn golden in 30 seconds when the oil is hot enough.) Fry the eggs in the oil for 1 minute or until golden brown, then drain on paper towel.

Divide the asparagus spears among plates, place a fried egg on each, drizzle with olive oil and vinegar, season, then serve.
* Panko are coarse, light Japanese breadcrumbs from selected supermarkets and Asian food shops.

parmesan custards

Serves 4

When I worked in the food department of the famous London store, Harrods, many years ago, the gentry would buy beautiful little jars of Gentleman's Relish. It's a salty anchovy paste that goes well with eggs and, of course, toast. It's hard to find in Australia, but Vegemite works nearly as well.

300ml pure (thin) cream
300ml milk
1¼ cups (100g) finely grated parmesan
4 egg yolks
Freshly ground white pepper
Toast soldiers sandwiched with Gentleman's Relish*
    or Vegemite, to serve

Combine the cream, milk and parmesan in a saucepan. Stir over low heat until the cheese melts. Leave to cool completely.

Preheat the oven to 150°C.

Gently whisk the egg yolks into the cream mixture, then season with salt and white pepper. Strain the mixture through a sieve into a jug, pushing down on any solids. Divide among four 200ml ovenproof ramekins or ceramic bowls.

Place the ramekins in a roasting pan, then pour enough boiling water into the pan to come halfway up the sides of the dishes. Place in the oven and bake for 15-20 minutes until the custards are pale golden and just set, but still with a slight wobble. Serve warm with the toast soldiers.

* From selected gourmet food shops.

quail egg & pancetta tart

Serves 6

375g block puff pastry
100ml creme fraiche or sour cream
2 tbs grated parmesan
150g thinly sliced pancetta
8 quail eggs* or 5 small eggs
Chervil sprigs* or flat-leaf parsley leaves, to garnish

Preheat oven to 180ºC. Line a baking tray with baking paper.

Roll out the pastry on a lightly floured surface to form a 16cm x 30cm rectangle. Place the pastry on the prepared baking tray. Use a knife to lightly score a 1cm border around the edge of the pastry, taking care not to cut all the way through. Prick the area inside the border with a fork.

Mix creme fraiche and parmesan in a bowl and season with salt and pepper. Spread the mixture over the pastry inside the border. Lay pancetta over the tart base, then bake for 12 minutes or until the pancetta is crisp and the pastry is puffed and golden.

Lightly beat 1 egg. Remove the pastry from the oven and brush the border with the beaten egg. Break the remaining eggs, one at a time, into a cup and pour over the pancetta. Season with salt and pepper, then return to the oven for a further 3 minutes or until the eggwhites are set but yolks are still runny. Scatter with chervil or parsley, then slice and serve.
* Quail eggs are available from selected poultry suppliers and Asian food shops. Chervil is from selected greengrocers.

EGGS

spanish eggs

Serves 4

This makes a very special breakfast dish but also doubles
as a great midweek dinner. Jars of chargrilled or roasted red
capsicum are available in most supermarkets these days, and
are an easy shortcut if you don't have time to roast your own.

500g pontiac or desiree potatoes, peeled,
   cut into 2cm cubes
2¹/₂ tbs olive oil
1 red onion, thinly sliced
2 garlic cloves, finely chopped
1 chorizo sausage, cut into 2cm pieces
1¹/₂ tsp smoked paprika* (pimenton)
¹/₂ tsp ground cumin
280g jar chargrilled or roasted red capsicum*,
   drained, chopped
4 free-range eggs
1 tbs finely chopped flat-leaf parsley

Cook the potato in a pan of boiling salted water for 2-3 minutes
until just tender, then drain and set aside.
   Heat 2 tablespoons oil in a large frypan over medium heat.
Add the onion and cook, stirring, for 2-3 minutes until just soft.
Add the garlic, chorizo, potato, paprika and cumin and cook,
stirring, for a further 2-3 minutes until the chorizo and potato
start to crisp. Add the chargrilled capsicum, season well,
then cook over low heat until heated through.
   Meanwhile, brush a non-stick frypan with the remaining
2 teaspoons oil and place over medium heat. Break the eggs,
one at a time, into the pan. Cover with a lid and cook for 2 minutes
until the eggwhites are cooked but the yolks are still soft.
   Divide the potato mixture among warm plates, top with an egg,
sprinkle with parsley, season with salt and pepper, then serve.
* Smoked paprika is from gourmet shops and selected delis.
Chargrilled capsicum is from supermarkets (see Glossary).

cheat's blinis with jamon and figs

Makes 32

Pedro Ximénez is a rich, sticky sweet sherry – it's not cheap, but if you keep a bottle on hand you can use it to add a special touch to desserts as well as this elegant canapé.

16 dried dessert figs, halved
¼ cup (60ml) Pedro Ximénez sherry or other sweet sherry
2 x 140g packets pikelet bites*
250g mascarpone cheese
100g sliced jamon serrano* or prosciutto, cut into strips
Olive oil, to drizzle
Chervil* or flat-leaf parsley sprigs, to garnish

Soak the figs in the sherry for 2 hours or until they have absorbed all the liquid.

Place the pikelets on a platter and spread each with a little mascarpone. Add a small scroll of jamon and a piece of fig. Sprinkle with sea salt and freshly ground black pepper, drizzle over oil and garnish with chervil or parsley.
* Pikelet bites are from supermarkets (see Glossary). Jamon serrano is Spanish cured ham from supermarkets and delis. Chervil is from selected greengrocers.

french goat's cheese dip

Serves 4-6

I'm a fan of goat's cheese but if you're not, cream cheese works equally well in this recipe. This dip can be used as a stuffing for roast chicken, too. Simply create a pocket between the skin and the breast, then carefully place the cheese mixture under the skin.

300g soft goat's cheese
1 tbs white wine vinegar
1 tbs dry white wine
2 tbs extra virgin olive oil
2 garlic cloves, crushed
2 tbs finely chopped flat-leaf parsley
2 tbs chopped chives
Baby (Dutch) carrots, celery sticks, radishes
    and crusty bread, to serve

Place the goat's cheese, vinegar, wine, oil, garlic, parsley and chives in a bowl with some sea salt and freshly ground black pepper. Beat well with a fork (or process in a food processor) until smooth, then serve with vegetables to dip and crusty bread.

quail eggs with walnut hummus and dukkah

Serves 4 as a snack

I love to make this dish as a simple starter or light lunch.

$^1/_2$ cup (60g) chopped toasted walnuts
250g tub hummus
2 tbs sour cream
1 tbs chopped flat-leaf parsley
12 quail eggs*
Roasted cherry truss tomatoes
    and warm pita bread, to serve
Walnut oil* or olive oil, to drizzle
$^1/_2$ cup dukkah*
Mint leaves, to garnish

Place the walnuts in a food processor and pulse to form fine crumbs. Add the hummus, sour cream and parsley, then pulse to combine.

Place the eggs in a saucepan of cold water and bring to the boil, then boil for 4 minutes. Peel the eggs under cold running water while still warm.

Place the hummus mixture and eggs on a serving plate with the cherry tomatoes. Drizzle with oil and sprinkle with the dukkah. Garnish with mint and serve with warm pita.
* Quail eggs are from selected poultry shops and delis. Dukkah (a spice, nut and seed blend) and walnut oil are from delis and gourmet shops.

chicken liver paté with rustic croutons

Serves 4-6

Chef Sean Moran of Sean's Panaroma, Bondi, serves these rustic croutons with patés and terrines – such a great idea!

400g unsalted butter
500g chicken livers, trimmed
2 eschalots, finely chopped
2 tbs each brandy and thickened cream
2 tbs black peppercorns
2 gold-strength gelatine leaves*
½ cup (125ml) chicken stock
1 loaf woodfired bread, crusts removed, torn into large chunks
2 tbs extra virgin olive oil
Onion marmalade*, to serve

Melt 100g butter in a pan over medium-high heat. Add the livers and cook for 2-3 minutes, turning once, until browned but still pink in the centre (be careful as it may spit). Transfer livers to a processor with tongs, then return frypan and butter to medium heat. Add eschalot and cook, stirring, for 2 minutes, then transfer to the processor. Add the brandy to the frypan and cook for 1 minute, scraping the pan to deglaze. Add to the processor with the cream and process to a rough paste.

Chop remaining 300g butter. With motor running, add 1 piece at a time until a smooth paste. Season, then push through a sieve into 2 ramekins or 1 larger terrine. Scatter with peppercorns. Chill while you make topping. Soften gelatine in cold water for 5 minutes. Warm stock over low heat. Squeeze excess water from gelatine, then add to stock and stir to dissolve. Cool. Pour over paté, cover and chill for at least 4 hours, or overnight, to set.

For the croutons, preheat the oven to 200°C and toss bread with olive oil on a baking tray. Toast for 10 minutes until crisp.

Serve the paté with the croutons and onion marmalade.
* From gourmet shops. Check gelatine pack for setting directions.

SMALL TASTES

posh popcorn

Makes 6 cups

If I'm feeling really posh, I use French butter from the deli, which adds a special flavour to the corn.

80g unsalted butter, chopped
3 garlic cloves, bruised
¼ cup (60ml) light olive oil
1 cup (230g) popcorn kernels
2 tbs herbes de Provence*
2 tsp celery salt

Melt the butter in a pan over low heat. Add the garlic and remove from heat. Set aside for 15 minutes to infuse.

Heat the oil in a large saucepan over high heat. Add the popcorn and toss to coat. Cover and shake the pan over the heat for 2-3 minutes until all the corn has popped.

Remove the garlic from the butter, then pour the butter over the popcorn. Add the herbs de Provence and celery salt, season with salt and pepper and toss to coat.

* Herbes de Provence is a dried herb mixture (including celery seed, parsley, thyme, tarragon, marjoram, bay and lavender flowers) from selected supermarkets and delis (see Glossary).

tuna sashimi with wasabi bean salad

Serves 4

Pick up some plastic soy sauce 'fish' at your local sushi bar
– it's fun to give each guest one to drizzle over their plate.

1-2 tsp wasabi paste (to taste), plus extra to serve
1 tbs red wine vinegar
2 tsp lemon juice
2½ tbs olive oil
350g thin green beans
1 small red onion, thinly sliced
Handful flat-leaf parsley leaves, torn
225g sashimi-grade tuna*, thinly sliced
Black* or regular sesame seeds, to sprinkle
Soy sauce, to serve

Combine the wasabi, vinegar and lemon juice in a bowl.
Gradually whisk in the oil until well combined.
   Slice the beans using an old-fashioned beaner (from
kitchenware shops) or slice on an angle. Blanch in a pan
of boiling salted water for 1 minute until just tender,
then drain, refresh in cold water and drain again.
   Toss the beans, onion and parsley in a bowl with the wasabi
dressing. Divide the beans among small bowls, then place on
serving plates with the tuna. Sprinkle with sesame seeds,
then serve with soy sauce and a dab of extra wasabi.
* Sashimi-grade tuna is from fishmongers. Black sesame seeds
are from Asian food shops.

beetroot & goat's cheese stacks

Serves 4

425g can sliced beetroot, drained
¼ cup (60ml) olive oil
¼ cup (60ml) balsamic vinegar
3 tsp chopped chives
2 tbs milk
120g soft goat's cheese
Micro salad and herb leaves* or regular mixed
    baby salad leaves, to garnish
2 tbs toasted chopped walnuts

Choose 12 even-sized slices of beetroot, pat dry with paper
towel, then lay in a shallow dish. Cover with the oil and
balsamic, then set aside at room temperature for 1 hour.

Place the chives, milk and goat's cheese in a bowl. Season
with salt and pepper, then mash with a fork until smooth.

Just before serving, drain beetroot (reserving dressing) and
pat slices dry with paper towel. Place 1 slice of beetroot on
a serving plate. Spoon the cheese mixture into a piping bag
and pipe some onto the beetroot (alternatively, spread about
1 tablespoon of the mixture over the beetroot with the back
of a spoon). Repeat with more beetroot and cheese, then
finish with a final beetroot slice. Repeat to make 4 stacks.

Garnish each stack with a few leaves, sprinkle some
walnuts around each plate, then drizzle with the reserved
dressing. Serve immediately.
* Available from selected greengrocers and growers' markets.

deep-fried brie with sweet chilli sauce

Serves 4

Back in the '70s, everyone served deep-fried brie as a starter. Extra crunchy panko breadcrumbs and sweet chilli sauce add a new dimension to this classic.

2 cups panko breadcrumbs* or coarse fresh breadcrumbs
Finely grated zest of 1 lemon
2 tbs chopped flat-leaf parsley
2 tbs plain flour
1 egg, beaten
2 tbs milk
350g piece brie or camembert, cut into 4 wedges
Sunflower oil, to deep-fry
Sweet chilli sauce and wild rocket leaves, to serve

Place the breadcrumbs in a food processor with the lemon zest and parsley, then pulse to fine crumbs. Place the crumb mixture in a shallow bowl, place the flour in a separate bowl, and gently whisk the egg and milk in a third bowl

Toss the wedges of cheese first in the flour, shaking off excess, then in the egg mixture, then in the breadcrumbs. Place on a plate and chill for at least 30 minutes (or up to 4 hours ahead).

Half-fill a deep-fryer or large heavy-based saucepan with oil and heat to 190°C. (If you don't have a deep-fryer thermometer, test a cube of bread – it'll turn golden in 30 seconds when the oil is hot enough.) Deep-fry the cheese for 1 minute or until golden all over, then drain briefly on paper towel.
Serve immediately with sweet chilli sauce and rocket.
* Coarse, light Japanese breadcrumbs from Asian food shops.

salmon & prawn timbales with chilli cucumber

Serves 4

16 slices smoked salmon
16 cooked prawns, peeled, deveined, chopped
1 cup (250g) sour cream or creme fraiche
2 tbs chopped coriander
1 tbs finely grated lemon zest
1 Lebanese cucumber
1 long red chilli, seeds removed, finely chopped
¼ cup (60ml) peanut oil
2 tsp soy sauce
1 tsp white wine vinegar
1 tsp caster sugar

Line four ½ cup (125ml) ramekins or coffee cups with plastic wrap, leaving some overhanging. Line each with 4 salmon slices, leaving enough overhanging to enclose.

Place the prawns, sour cream, coriander and lemon zest in a food processor, season with salt and pepper and pulse to combine. Fill the ramekins with the prawn mixture, cover with the overhanging salmon and enclose with the wrap. Chill for 4 hours until firm.

Meanwhile, use a peeler to shave long strips from the cucumber, turning as you go. Discard the seeds in the centre. Place the chilli and oil in a small saucepan over low heat. Add the soy, vinegar and sugar and stir to dissolve the sugar. Season, cool slightly, then add cucumber to the chilli dressing. Cover and chill for 30 minutes to marinate.

Unmould the timbales onto serving plates, top with chilli cucumber and drizzle with any remaining dressing.

roasted cherry tomato tarte tatins

Serves 4

4 x 190g jars roasted cherry tomatoes in oil*,
  drained, oil reserved
4 frozen puff pastry sheets, thawed
100g Persian feta*, crumbled
2 tbs small basil leaves, to garnish
Balsamic vinegar, to drizzle

Preheat the oven to 180°C. Lightly grease four 12cm blini pans
or small non-stick pie dishes with some of the reserved oil.

  Arrange cherry tomatoes in a single layer over the base of
each pan, packing in close together, to completely cover.

  Cut 4 circles from the pastry, slightly larger than the base
of the pans. Place pastry over the tomatoes, tucking in the
edges. Place on a tray and bake for 20 minutes or until the
pastry is puffed and golden.

  Remove the tarts from the oven and stand for 10 minutes,
then turn out onto serving plates. Scatter with the feta and
garnish with basil. Serve drizzled with balsamic and a little
more of the reserved oil.

* Roasted cherry tomatoes in oil (see Glossary) are from
supermarkets and delis. Persian feta is available from
delis and gourmet shops.

hummus soup

Serves 4-6

I love hummus, so why not make it a soup?
This makes a lovely starter for a Moroccan meal.

1L (4 cups) chicken stock
3 garlic cloves, finely chopped
Grated zest and juice of 1 small lemon,
    plus wedges to serve
2 x 400g cans chickpeas, rinsed, drained
1 tbs chopped mint leaves
1 tbs chopped flat-leaf parsley leaves
Natural yoghurt, to drizzle
Extra virgin olive oil, to drizzle
2 tbs dukkah*
Flatbread, to serve

Place the stock in a saucepan with the garlic, lemon zest and
chickpeas and bring to the boil over medium-high heat. Reduce
heat to medium-low and simmer for 5 minutes. Cool slightly,
then add the mint, parsley and lemon juice and puree using a
stick blender (or puree in batches in a blender) until smooth.
   Season to taste with salt and pepper, then reheat over low heat.
Ladle soup into serving bowls, drizzle over yoghurt and oil and
sprinkle with dukkah. Serve with lemon wedges and flatbread.
* Dukkah is a spice, nut and seed blend from delis and
Middle Eastern food shops.

chilled cucumber soup with smoked trout tartines

Serves 4-6

30g unsalted butter, plus extra softened butter to spread
1 onion, chopped
4 telegraph cucumbers, peeled, seeds removed, chopped
200g pontiac or desiree potatoes, peeled, chopped
3 cups (750ml) chicken stock
3 dill sprigs, roughly chopped
200g creme fraiche
2 ficelle* loaves (or 1 baguette)
500g smoked trout, flaked
Mustard cress or rocket leaves, to garnish

Melt the butter in a saucepan over medium-low heat. Add the onion and cook, stirring, for 3-4 minutes until softened but not coloured. Add the cucumber, potato and stock, then season with salt and pepper. Bring to the boil, then simmer over medium low heat for 20 minutes or until the potato is tender.

Cool slightly, then add the dill. Puree using a stick blender (or puree in batches in a blender) until smooth. Whisk in the creme fraiche and allow to cool. Cover and refrigerate for at least 4 hours until well chilled.

Just before serving, split the ficelle lengthways and spread with the softened butter. Fill with the smoked trout and season, then garnish with cress or rocket. Slice into 2-3 pieces each. Serve the chilled soup in bowls with trout tartines on the side.
* A ficelle is a thin half-baguette available from selected bakeries.

spiced carrot & lentil soup

Serves 4-6

2 tsp cumin seeds
Pinch of dried chilli flakes
2 tbs olive oil
1 onion, chopped
5 carrots (600g total), roughly chopped
¾ cup (150g) red lentils
1L (4 cups) chicken stock
150ml pure (thin) cream, plus extra to serve

Heat a large saucepan over low heat. Add the cumin and chilli flakes and cook, stirring, for 1 minute until fragrant. Remove half the spice mixture and set aside to garnish.

Increase heat to medium and add the oil to the pan. Cook the onion, stirring, for 3-4 minutes until the onion starts to soften. Add the carrot, lentils and stock and bring to the boil. Reduce heat to medium-low and simmer for 15-20 minutes until carrot is tender. Cool slightly, then puree using a stick blender (or puree in batches in a blender) until smooth.

Return to the pan and season with salt and pepper. Stir in the cream and reheat gently over low heat. Serve drizzled with extra cream, scattered with the reserved spices.

bean, coconut & lime soup

Serves 4-6

1 tbs sunflower oil
1 onion, chopped
1-2 tsp Thai green curry paste or jungle curry paste
2 x 400g cans cannellini beans, rinsed, drained
350ml chicken stock
2 kaffir lime leaves*
Zest and juice of 1 lime
400ml coconut milk
2 tsp fish sauce
Sliced red chilli, coriander leaves and
    chopped peanuts, to serve

Heat the oil in a saucepan over medium heat. Add the onion and cook, stirring occasionally, for 1-2 minutes until soft. Add the curry paste and cook, stirring, for 1 minute or until fragrant. Add the beans, stock, lime leaves, zest and juice. Increase the heat to medium-high and bring to the boil, then reduce the heat to low and simmer for 10 minutes.

Cool slightly, then remove and discard the lime leaves. Puree using a stick blender (or puree in batches in a blender) until smooth, then stir in the coconut milk and fish sauce. Reheat gently over low heat. Ladle into serving bowls and sprinkle with chilli, coriander and peanuts.
* From greengrocers and Asian food shops.

pea soup with croque monsieur

Serves 4-6

A toasted croque monsieur sandwich filled with ham, mustard and gruyere turns this soup into a great midweek dinner. Or, for a dinner party, cut smaller circles from the sandwiches and serve as a crouton in the soup.

1 tbs olive oil
20g unsalted butter
1 onion, chopped
2 celery stalks, chopped
1 leek (pale part only), thinly sliced
1 potato, peeled, chopped
1 bouquet garni*
2 cups (500ml) chicken stock
2 cups (240g) frozen peas (not baby)
½ cup (125ml) pure (thin) cream
½ cup mint leaves, chopped
Snow pea sprouts, to garnish
Toasted croque monsieur sandwiches or croutons, to serve

Heat oil and butter in a pan over medium heat. Add onion, celery and leek and cook, stirring, for 5 minutes or until vegetables are soft but not browned. Add potato, bouquet garni and stock and simmer for 5 minutes until potato is soft. Add peas and cream and simmer for a further minute, then remove 2-3 tablespoons peas with a slotted spoon and set aside.

Puree using a stick blender (or puree in batches in a blender) until smooth. Return the reserved peas to the pan and reheat soup gently over low heat. Serve soup in bowls with a croque monsieur in the centre, if desired, garnished with snow pea sprouts.

* Bouquet garni is a bunch of herbs (usually parsley, thyme and bay leaves) tied with string and used to flavour soups and stews. Make your own fresh, or buy ready-made dried bouquet garni from delis and selected supermarkets (see Glossary).

64

the chicken that thought it was christmas

Serves 4

I love the flavours of Christmas and make any excuse throughout the year to cook up a mini festive roast.

8 slices pancetta or bacon	**Bread sauce**
4 spatchcocks*, trussed with kitchen string	30g unsalted butter
1 tbs olive oil	1 large onion, finely chopped
150ml dry red wine	100ml pure (thin) cream
150ml chicken stock	1 bay leaf
4 tbs redcurrant jelly	5 cloves
Fresh breadcrumbs fried in butter, to serve (optional)	1½ cups (100g) fresh white breadcrumbs
	300ml milk
	Pinch of nutmeg

Preheat the oven to 180°C. Cross 2 pancetta slices over each spatchcock, season and drizzle with oil. Roast for 40 minutes or until the juices run clear when the thigh is pierced.

While spatchcocks are roasting, make sauce. Melt butter in a pan over low heat. Add onion and cook for 5 minutes or until softened. Add cream, bay and cloves and stir for 2-3 minutes. Remove from heat and stand for 20 minutes to infuse. Discard bay and cloves, then puree in a food processor and set aside. Simmer crumbs and milk in a pan on low heat for 5-6 minutes, stirring, until smooth. Add onion puree and nutmeg, then season. Cover surface of the sauce with baking paper.

Remove birds from pan and leave to rest while you make a gravy. Place roasting pan on the stove over medium heat. Add wine, stock and jelly, then simmer, stirring and scraping pan, for 5-6 minutes until gravy thickens. Serve spatchcocks with gravy and bread sauce, topped with extra crumbs if desired.

* From poultry shops and selected supermarkets.

easy coq au vin

Serves 4

Using flavoursome thigh fillet instead of whole chicken pieces is a great way to speed up a classic coq au vin.

8 eschalots, peeled
1 tbs olive oil
60g sliced pancetta, cut into strips
8 chicken thigh fillets, cut into 3cm pieces
2 tbs plain flour
3 garlic cloves, finely chopped
150g button mushrooms, quartered
2 tbs tomato paste
1 cup (250ml) good-quality chicken stock
  or chicken consommé
1 cup (250ml) dry red wine
1 tbs chopped fresh thyme leaves
2 bay leaves
Chopped flat-leaf parsley and toasted baguette, to serve

Par-cook the eschalots in boiling water for 5 minutes, then drain and set aside.

Heat the oil in a large deep frypan or casserole pan over medium heat. Add pancetta and cook, stirring, for 2-3 minutes until starting to crisp. Season chicken, then add to the pan and cook for 5-6 minutes until lightly browned. Add flour and stir to coat chicken, then stir in the garlic, mushrooms and tomato paste.

Once everything is well combined, add the stock, wine, thyme, bay leaves and eschalots. Season well, bring to the boil, then reduce heat to medium-low and simmer for 20 minutes or until the chicken is cooked through and the sauce has thickened.

Serve the coq au vin in deep bowls with parsley and toasted baguette to mop up the lovely sauce.

oregano chicken on bean & olive salad

Serves 4

I like to use the branches of dried oregano found in Greek delis and Middle Eastern food shops, as the flavour is so much better than regular dried oregano.

2 tbs dried oregano leaves
1 tsp dried red chilli flakes
Zest and juice of 1 lemon, plus lemon to serve
1/2 cup (125ml) extra virgin olive oil
4 corn-fed chicken breasts with skin*
   (wingbone attached, optional)
450g waxy potatoes (such as Anya or kipfler)
300g thin green beans, topped
1 small red onion, thinly sliced
2 tbs chopped flat-leaf parsley
100g pitted kalamata olives, crushed
2 tsp red wine vinegar

Mix the oregano, chilli, lemon zest and juice and 1/3 cup (80ml) of the oil in a bowl with salt and pepper. Make a few slashes in the chicken skin, then place chicken in a shallow dish and rub in the marinade, making sure it's well coated. Cover and marinate in the fridge for 1-2 hours.

   Meanwhile, make the salad. Boil the potatoes in a pan of salted water for 8-10 minutes until just tender. Drain, return to the pan and lightly crush. Blanch the beans in boiling salted water for 2 minutes, then drain. Place in a large bowl with the crushed potatoes, remaining oil, onion, parsley, olives and vinegar. Season well, then set aside while you cook the chicken.

   Meanwhile, preheat a chargrill pan or barbecue on medium-high. Grill the chicken for 5-6 minutes each side until cooked through (if browning too quickly, finish cooking in the oven).

   Serve the chicken on the salad, with extra lemon to squeeze.
* Available from poultry shops and butchers.

chicken, leek & bacon pot pies

Serves 4

40g unsalted butter
1 tbs olive oil
3 leeks (pale part only), thinly sliced
4 bacon rashers, rind removed, chopped
800g chicken thigh fillets, cut into 2cm pieces
1 tbs plain flour
Pinch of nutmeg
200ml chicken stock
300ml light sour cream or creme fraiche
2 tbs chopped flat-leaf parsley
2 tbs lemon juice
4 sheets frozen puff pastry
1 egg, lightly beaten

Heat the butter and oil in a pan over low heat. Add the leek, bacon and chicken and cook, stirring, for 6-8 minutes until the leek is soft and chicken is almost cooked. Stir in the flour and nutmeg and cook for 1-2 minutes until the chicken is cooked through. Stir in the stock, increase heat to medium and bring to the boil. Season, then remove from the heat and stir in the sour cream, parsley and lemon juice. Cool completely.

Preheat the oven to 200°C.

Cut two 1cm strips from the sides of each pastry sheet. Set aside. Cut pie lids from the remaining pastry, 1cm wider than the top of four 300ml pie dishes or ramekins. Divide chicken mixture among dishes. Press pastry strips around the rim of each dish to make a 'collar' and brush with some of the egg. Carefully top with pie lids, press firmly into the collar to seal, then trim edges if necessary. Make 2 cuts in each pie top, then brush with remaining egg. Bake the pies for 20 minutes or until puffed and golden.

CHICKEN

chicken with chilli chocolate

Serves 4

This easy version of the classic Mexican mole stew uses good-quality chilli chocolate to add depth and spice to the sauce.

1 tbs olive oil
20g unsalted butter
4 chicken breast fillets
100g pancetta, cut into strips
2 celery stalks, chopped
1 onion, sliced
2 garlic cloves, finely chopped
150ml dry red wine
400ml chicken stock
400g can chopped tomatoes
50g chilli chocolate*, broken into small pieces
300g can red kidney beans, rinsed, drained
Steamed rice, sliced red chilli, coriander leaves (optional),
    corn chips and avocado wedges, to serve

Preheat the oven to 180°C.
   Heat the oil and butter in a casserole pan over medium heat. Add the chicken and cook for 2-3 minutes each side until golden, then remove and set aside. Add the pancetta, celery and onion and cook, stirring, for 5 minutes until vegetables soften. Add the garlic and wine and simmer for 2-3 minutes. Stir in the stock, tomato and chocolate, then return chicken to the pan. Cover and transfer to the oven for 25 minutes or until the chicken is cooked through.
   Remove chicken from the pan, cover loosely with foil and set aside in a warm place. Return the pan to the stove over medium-high heat, add the beans and simmer for 4-5 minutes until thickened. Slice the chicken and serve on steamed rice, with the sauce, chilli, and coriander if desired. Serve with corn chips and avocado.
* Available from supermarkets (see Glossary).

CHICKEN

rosemary lamb kebabs with lemon & olive relish

Serves 4

If you have a rosemary bush, strip most of the leaves from 4 long, thin branches to use as skewers.

2 garlic cloves, finely chopped
2 tbs olive oil
1 tbs chopped rosemary leaves
1 tbs paprika, plus extra to dust
1 tbs lemon juice
500g lamb fillet, cut into 2cm cubes
4 vine-ripened tomatoes, seeds removed, chopped
1 tbs chopped preserved lemon rind*
   (white pith and flesh discarded)
2 tbs chopped pitted kalamata olives
2 tbs chopped flat-leaf parsley
Thick Greek-style yoghurt, to serve

Soak 4 rosemary branches or bamboo skewers in cold water for 30 minutes to prevent them from burning.
   Combine the garlic, oil, rosemary, paprika and lemon juice in a glass or ceramic dish. Season well, then add the lamb, tossing to coat well. Cover and marinate in the fridge for 1-2 hours.
   Meanwhile, combine the tomato, preserved lemon rind, olives and parsley in a bowl. Season to taste (it will already be quite salty from the lemon), then set the relish aside.
   Thread the lamb onto the branches or skewers. Heat a chargrill pan or barbecue on medium-high heat. Cook the lamb, turning occasionally, for 6-8 minutes until browned all over but still juicy in the centre. Serve the skewers with the relish and yoghurt, dusted with a little extra paprika.
* Available from gourmet food shops and delis.

porcini-dusted lamb with cheat's mushroom "risotto"

Serves 4

I often substitute risoni pasta for arborio rice when I am short on time – it's quicker to cook and there's no need to stir.

5 tbs (30g) porcini powder*
4 x 200g lamb backstraps, well-trimmed
2 tbs olive oil, plus extra to brush
300g Swiss brown mushrooms
1 tsp rosemary leaves
2 garlic cloves, crushed
1/2 cup (125ml) dry white wine
1 cup (220g) risoni pasta (orzo)
2 cups (500ml) chicken stock
3/4 cup (60g) grated parmesan
Rocket leaves, to serve

Spread 4 tablespoons of the porcini powder in a shallow dish. Brush lamb with extra oil, then season and roll in the powder. Heat 1 tablespoon oil in a deep frypan over medium-high heat. Cook the lamb, turning, for 3 minutes each side for medium-rare (or until done to your liking). Remove from the pan, cover loosely with foil, and keep warm in a low oven while you make the risotto.

Heat remaining oil in a large non-stick frypan over medium heat. Add mushrooms, rosemary and garlic and cook, stirring, for 3-4 minutes until mushrooms are just tender. Add the wine, risoni and stock, then bring to the boil. Reduce heat to low and simmer for 8-10 minutes until all stock is absorbed and risoni is al dente. Stir in the parmesan and remaining porcini powder and season. Thickly slice the lamb and serve on the risoni with rocket.
* Porcini powder is from gourmet food shops (see Glossary). If you can't find it, grind dried porcini mushrooms in a coffee grinder.

dukkah-crusted lamb with radish tzatziki

Serves 4

1 tbs pomegranate molasses*, plus extra to drizzle
1 tbs honey, warmed
1 cup dukkah*
12 French-trimmed lamb cutlets
1 tbs olive oil
6 radishes, trimmed
1 telegraph cucumber
250g thick Greek-style yoghurt
2 garlic cloves, crushed
2 tbs chopped mint, plus leaves to garnish
Fresh pomegranate seeds* (optional), to garnish

Preheat the oven to 180°C.

Combine molasses and honey in a bowl, and spread the dukkah in a separate shallow bowl.

Season cutlets with salt and pepper. Heat the oil in a frypan over medium-high heat and cook the cutlets, in 2 batches, for 1 minute each side until sealed. Brush the cutlets with the molasses mixture, then dip in the dukkah to coat. Place on a lined baking tray and cook in the oven for a further 5 minutes until cooked but still pink in the centre.

Meanwhile, coarsely grate the radishes and cucumber. Transfer to a sieve and squeeze out excess moisture. Combine with yoghurt, garlic and mint, then season with salt and pepper.

Drizzle the extra pomegranate molasses over the cutlets and garnish with pomegranate seeds. Serve with the tzatziki, garnished with extra mint leaves.

* Pomegranate molasses (see Glossary) and dukkah (a spice, nut and seed blend) are from Middle Eastern shops and delis. Pomegranates are available from greengrocers in season.

oven-baked
lamb curry

Serves 4

I like to serve this with crispy pappadams or naan bread.

600g lamb fillets, cut into 2cm cubes
2 tbs olive oil
1 onion, thinly sliced
2 tbs mild curry paste (such as korma)
600ml chicken or vegetable stock
400g can chopped tomatoes
2 cinnamon quills
2 garlic cloves, finely chopped
12 fresh curry leaves*
1⅓ cups (300g) medium-grain rice
Natural yoghurt, to serve

Preheat the oven to 180°C.

Season the lamb. Heat half the oil in a frypan over medium-high heat. Brown the lamb, in batches, for 2-3 minutes, then remove and set aside.

Return the pan to medium heat with the remaining oil. Add the onion and cook, stirring, for 5 minutes until golden. Add the curry paste and stir for a few seconds until fragrant, then transfer to a 2.5-litre baking dish. Add the lamb, stock, tomato, cinnamon, garlic and curry leaves. Season with salt and pepper, stir well to combine, then cover with foil and bake for 20 minutes.

Stir the rice into the curry, then return to the oven, uncovered, for 10 minutes or until the lamb is tender and the rice is cooked. Serve the curry topped with yoghurt.

* Available from selected greengrocers and Asian food shops.

gnocchi-topped cottage pies

Serves 6

Update the classic cottage pie by swapping mashed potato
for a golden gnocchi topping.

2 tbs olive oil, plus extra to toss
100g sliced pancetta or bacon, chopped
1 large onion, chopped
2 small carrots, chopped
1 tbs plain flour
4 garlic cloves, chopped
1 tbs tomato paste
1kg lamb mince
300ml dry red wine
2 cups (500ml) beef stock
2 bay leaves
2 tsp chopped thyme
2 x 500g packets potato gnocchi
40g unsalted butter, melted
2 tbs grated parmesan

Heat the oil in a large frypan over medium heat. Add the pancetta,
onion and carrot and cook, stirring, for 5 minutes or until the
onion has softened. Add the flour, garlic and paste and cook,
stirring, for a further minute. Add the mince and cook for
5-6 minutes until well browned. Add the wine, stock, bay leaves
and thyme, season, then bring to the boil. Reduce the heat to
low and simmer for 1 hour or until sauce has thickened. Cool.
   Preheat the oven to 190°C.
   Cook the gnocchi according to packet instructions. Drain,
then toss in a little olive oil.
   Divide the lamb mixture among six 400ml ovenproof dishes
and cover the top of each with gnocchi. Brush the tops with
the melted butter, then sprinkle with parmesan. Bake the
pies for 20 minutes or until golden.

new beef stroganoff

Serves 4

4 x 180g beef fillet steaks
¼ cup (60ml) olive oil, plus extra to brush
2 tbs mixed dried peppercorns, crushed
250g Swiss brown mushrooms, sliced
2 tbs brandy
1¼ cups (310ml) beef stock
1 tbs Dijon mustard
¼ cup chopped flat-leaf parsley,
    plus extra to serve
½ cup (125ml) thickened cream
400g pappardelle or fettuccine

Brush the steaks with a little oil, then season with salt. Sprinkle all over with the crushed peppercorns, gently pressing into the steaks. Heat 1 tablespoon oil in a frypan over medium-high heat. Add the steaks and cook for 2-3 minutes each side until well-seared but still rare in the centre (or until cooked to your liking). Set aside and cover loosely with foil to keep warm.

Add the remaining oil to the steak pan. Add mushrooms and cook, stirring, for 3 minutes until they start to soften. Add the brandy and stock, then bring to the boil. Decrease the heat to medium-low and simmer for 5 minutes or until reduced by half. Stir in the mustard, parsley and cream. Cook for a further minute, stirring, until heated through.

Meanwhile, cook the pasta in a saucepan of boiling salted water according to packet instructions. Drain, then add to the pan with the sauce and toss to combine.

Slice the steak 1cm-thick on an angle, then divide among plates with the pasta. Drizzle with any sauce left in the pan, then serve garnished with parsley.

my pho

Serves 4

My version of the Vietnamese noodle soup, pho, is quick and easy – I just pick up some rare roast beef from the deli and lovely aromatic herbs from the greengrocer on my way home. Serve topped with chilli jam for a little extra heat.

200g flat rice-stick noodles
1 tbs sunflower oil
6 spring onions, sliced on an angle
2cm piece ginger, very thinly sliced
1 small red chilli, seeds removed, finely chopped
3 cups (750ml) beef consommé*
¼ cup (60ml) fish sauce
¼ cup (60ml) lime juice
100g bean sprouts, ends trimmed
¼ cup coriander leaves, plus extra to serve
¼ cup Thai basil leaves*, plus extra to serve
¼ cup mint leaves, plus extra to serve
400g thinly sliced rare roast beef

Soften the noodles in a bowl of boiling water according to packet instructions.

Meanwhile, heat the oil in a saucepan over medium heat. Add the spring onion, ginger and chilli and cook, stirring, for 2-3 minutes until onion is soft. Add the consommé and 1 cup (250ml) water, then bring to the boil. Decrease the heat to low and simmer for 10 minutes. Stir in the fish sauce and lime juice.

Divide the noodles, bean sprouts and herbs among soup bowls, then ladle over the broth. Serve topped with beef slices and extra herbs.

* Beef consommé is available in cans and tetra packs from supermarkets. Thai basil is available from greengrocers and Asian food shops; substitute regular basil.

thai-style braised beef cheeks

Serves 6

Don't be put off by the long list of ingredients – everything goes into the one pan so you can leave it in a slow-cooker or in the oven.

6 beef cheeks*
1/3 cup (50g) plain flour, seasoned
2 tbs sunflower oil
3 onions, sliced
4cm piece galangal*, sliced
1 lemongrass stem (pale part only), sliced
4cm piece fresh ginger, sliced into thin matchsticks
1/2 cup (135g) grated palm sugar* (or use brown sugar)
3 garlic cloves, sliced
3 kaffir lime leaves*

3 long red chillies, seeds removed, thinly sliced
1/3 cup tamarind puree*
2 cups (500ml) beef stock
1/2 cup (125ml) fish sauce
Steamed rice, to serve

Herb salad
2 cups mixed Asian herbs (such as coriander, Thai basil* and Vietnamese mint*)
6 spring onions, sliced into very thin strips
2 tbs olive oil
1 tbs lime juice

Coat the beef in flour, shaking off excess. Heat the oil in a large pan over medium-high heat. In 2 batches, brown the beef for 1-2 minutes each side. Transfer to a slow-cooker or flameproof casserole. Add 1 litre (4 cups) water and all the remaining ingredients, reserving 1 sliced chilli for the salad. Stir to combine, then cover and cook on low heat for 7 hours (or overnight) in a slow-cooker, or in the oven at 170°C for 3 hours 30 minutes until the beef is very tender. Remove the beef and set aside. Reduce liquid over medium-high heat until you have a thick sauce.

Just before serving, place the herb salad ingredients in a bowl with the remaining chilli, season with salt and toss to combine. Serve the beef on rice, topped with sauce and the herb salad.
* Order beef cheeks from your butcher. Substitute large pieces of chuck steak. All other ingredients are from Asian food shops.

steak with simple bearnaise

Serves 4

Use your blender to create this easy bearnaise sauce, instead of using the traditional double-boiler method. You can make the sauce up to 2 hours in advance and keep it warm in a thermos flask. Give it a good shake before pouring.

2 tbs tarragon vinegar*
1 eschalot, finely chopped
6 black peppercorns
2 tbs chopped tarragon leaves*
4 rib-eye steaks
2 tbs olive oil, to brush
3 egg yolks
140g unsalted butter
Watercress or rocket leaves, to serve
Shoestring fries, to serve

Place the vinegar, eschalot, peppercorns, half the tarragon leaves and 2 tablespoons water in a pan over medium heat and simmer for 1 minute until reduced to about 1 tablespoon of liquid. Strain through a fine sieve, pressing down on solids.

Brush the steaks with oil and season with salt and pepper. Heat a chargrill pan over high heat and cook the steaks for 3-4 minutes each side for medium-rare (or until cooked to your liking). Rest in a warm place, loosely covered with foil, for 5 minutes.

Meanwhile, place egg yolks and tarragon reduction in a blender and whiz to combine. Melt butter in a pan over medium-low heat. With the motor running, very slowly and carefully pour the butter through the feed tube of the blender while it's still hot and bubbling, to form a thick sauce. Stir in remaining tarragon. Drizzle sauce over steak, season and serve with watercress and fries.
* Tarragon vinegar is from delis and gourmet food shops.
Fresh tarragon is from selected greengrocers.

special steak tartare

Serves 4

For an extra treat, serve this dish with creme fraiche mixed with truffle oil (from gourmet food shops) and chopped chives.

400g good-quality beef eye fillet
2 eschalots, finely chopped
4 cornichons (small pickled cucumbers), finely chopped
2 anchovy fillets, finely chopped
1 tbs baby capers, rinsed, drained,
   finely chopped
1 tsp Dijon mustard
4 quail eggs*
4 green salad leaves
Olive oil, to drizzle
Good-quality potato crisps, to serve
Creme fraiche or truffled creme fraiche (optional), to serve

Cut the beef into wafer-thin slices. Place 3-4 pieces on top of each other and cut into strips, then very finely chop. Place in a bowl with the eschalot, cornichon, anchovy, caper and mustard. Separate the quail egg yolks from the whites. Stir 2 eggwhites into the beef mixture. Discard remaining eggwhites.

Place the leaves on a serving platter, then place a metal egg ring over each leaf and gently press the beef into the mould. Make a small indent in the centre of each and slide in an egg yolk. Sprinkle with pepper and drizzle with oil. Serve with the potato chips and creme fraiche, if desired.

* Available from selected poultry shops and Asian food shops.

quick italian-style roast pork

Serves 4

600g desiree potatoes, peeled, cut into 3cm chunks
2 tbs olive oil
1 rosemary sprig, leaves finely chopped
2 garlic cloves, finely chopped
2 pork fillets (about 500g each), halved
8 thin slices flat pancetta*
250g cherry truss tomatoes, separated into sprigs
Good-quality basil pesto, to serve

Preheat the oven to 200°C and grease a large baking tray.
  Blanch the potato for 5 minutes in boiling salted water,
then drain well. Spread on the tray, toss with 1 tablespoon
of oil, then season and roast for 20 minutes.
  Meanwhile, mix together the rosemary, garlic and remaining
tablespoon of oil. Coat the pork in the mixture, then wrap
2 slices of pancetta around each fillet and secure with kitchen
string or toothpicks. Season with salt and pepper. Add the pork
to the tray with the potatoes and roast for a further 15 minutes.
Add the tomatoes to the tray, then season and return to the
oven for a further 5 minutes until the potato is golden, the
pork is cooked and the tomatoes are just starting to soften.
  Serve the roast pork and vegetables with pesto to drizzle.
* Flat pancetta is from selected delis and butchers.

sticky honey, soy & ginger pork ribs

Serves 3-4

5cm piece fresh ginger, grated
6 garlic cloves, finely chopped
1/2 cup (125ml) light soy sauce
1/2 cup (175g) honey
1/2 cup (125ml) Chinese rice wine (shaohsing)*
1 tbs sweet chilli sauce
1.4kg pork ribs, cut into individual ribs
Coriander, lime wedges and steamed rice, to serve

Combine the ginger, garlic, soy, honey, rice wine and sweet chilli sauce in a large zip-lock bag. Add the ribs, close the bag and shake to coat the pork thoroughly. Marinate in the fridge for at least 1 hour or overnight.

Preheat the oven to 180°C.

Remove the ribs from the bag, reserving the marinade, and place on a rack over a roasting pan filled with 1cm water. Roast for 35-40 minutes until sticky and golden. Remove the pork from the rack and set aside, loosely covered with foil, while you make the glaze.

For the glaze, place the marinade in a small saucepan over medium-high heat with any juices from the roasting pan. Bring to the boil, then allow to bubble for 4-5 minutes until the mixture is sticky, watching carefully to ensure it doesn't burn. Brush over the ribs.

Place the glazed ribs on a serving platter with coriander and lime wedges, then serve with steamed rice.
* From Asian food shops; substitute dry sherry.

stir-fried pork wraps

Serves 4

Small flour tortillas make a perfect wrap for this quick
pork stir-fry – a favourite TV dinner in my home.

8 dried shiitake mushrooms*
1 tbs sesame oil
2 tbs peanut oil
300g pork mince
¼ cup (60ml) light soy sauce
2 tbs Chinese rice wine (shaohsing)* or dry sherry
2 tsp caster sugar
2 tbs grated fresh ginger
1 small red onion, thinly sliced
¼ savoy cabbage, very thinly sliced
2 tbs plum sauce, plus extra to serve
1 tbs chopped mint leaves, plus extra leaves to serve
2 carrots, thinly sliced into matchsticks
1 Lebanese cucumber, thinly sliced into matchsticks
8 small flour tortillas, warmed according to packet instructions

Soak the dried mushrooms in ¼ cup (60ml) boiling water
for 10 minutes, then slice. Reserve the soaking liquid.
   Heat the oils in a wok over medium-high heat. Add the pork
and stir-fry, breaking up with a spoon, for 3-4 minutes until
lightly browned. Add the soy sauce, rice wine, sugar, ginger,
onion, cabbage, plum sauce, chopped mint and shiitakes
and stir-fry for a further 2-3 minutes until cabbage wilts.
   Serve the pork, vegetables, warm tortillas and extra mint and
plum sauce separately, for people to make their own wraps.
* From Asian food shops and selected supermarkets.

spanish pork with orange & poppyseed salad

Serves 4

1 tsp cumin
1 tbs smoked paprika* (pimenton)
Zest and juice of 1 orange
1/3 cup (80ml) tomato sauce (ketchup)
1/3 cup (80ml) maple syrup
2 pork fillets (about 500g each), trimmed, halved

Orange & poppyseed salad
2 oranges
3 Lebanese cucumbers, halved lengthways,
   seeds removed, sliced
1/4 cup coriander leaves
2 long red chillies, seeds removed, finely chopped
1/3 cup (80ml) white wine vinegar
1/2 cup (125ml) olive oil
2 tbs caster sugar
2 tbs poppyseeds

Combine all the ingredients in a zip-lock bag and shake well to coat pork. Marinate in the fridge for at least 1 hour or overnight.

For the salad, zest the rind of 1 orange and set aside in a small bowl. Peel both oranges, then halve and slice the flesh. Place in a large bowl with the cucumber, coriander and chilli. Add the vinegar, oil, sugar and poppyseeds to the zest bowl, season well and whisk to combine. Set salad and dressing aside.

Preheat a chargrill pan or barbecue on medium-high heat. Cook the pork, turning, for 5-6 minutes until blackened on the outside and cooked through. Set aside loosely covered with foil for 5 minutes to rest, then slice. Divide the salad mixture among 4 plates, top with the sliced pork, then drizzle with dressing.
* From gourmet food shops and selected delis.

PORK

crispy herbed pork cutlets

Serves 4

3 cups panko breadcrumbs*
1/2 cup (75g) plain flour, seasoned
1 tbs fresh lemon thyme (or regular thyme) leaves
3/4 cup (60g) grated parmesan
3 eggs, beaten
4 pork cutlets
1/4 cup (60ml) olive oil
30g unsalted butter
8 sage sprigs
Lemon wedges, to serve

Whiz the breadcrumbs in a food processor with the flour, thyme and parmesan to fine crumbs. Season with salt and pepper, then transfer to a shallow bowl. Place egg in a separate bowl.

Use a meat mallet to lightly pound the eye fillet of each pork cutlet to an even thickness. Dip the pork in the egg, then press into the crumb mixture to coat well all over.

Heat the oil in a large non-stick frypan over medium heat. Add the pork and fry for 2-3 minutes each side until golden and cooked through. Remove from the pan and set aside.

Add the butter and sage sprigs to the pan. When the butter begins to foam, return the pork to the pan and turn to coat in the buttery juices. Serve immediately with lemon wedges.

* Panko are light, crunchy Japanese breadcrumbs, available from Asian food shops and selected supermarkets.

fettuccine with sausage and peas

Serves 4

This is my version of chef Andy Bunn's recipe from
Cafe Sopra in Sydney. I love it because it has two of
my favourite ingredients, sausages and peas!

400g pork and herb sausages, casing removed
2 tbs chopped mint, plus extra leaves to garnish
2 cups (240g) frozen peas
250g mascarpone cheese
Juice of 1 lemon
2 tbs olive oil
500g fettuccine
2/3 cup (50g) grated parmesan

Combine the sausage meat and mint in a bowl. Roll into about
24 small (3cm) meatballs and chill until needed.
　Cook the peas in a pan of boiling salted water for 1–2 minutes
until tender. Drain, then return to the pan and crush with a fork.
Stir in mascarpone and lemon juice, then season and set aside.
　Heat the olive oil in a frypan over medium heat. Add the
meatballs in batches if necessary, and cook, turning, for
3-4 minutes until browned all over and cooked through.
　Meanwhile, cook the pasta according to packet instructions.
Drain, reserving 1 cup (250ml) of the cooking water. Add the
pasta and pea mixture to the meatball pan with enough of the
reserved water to form a sauce, then toss briefly to combine and
heat through. Stir in half the parmesan. Divide among bowls,
then serve topped with extra mint and remaining parmesan.

sausages with home-style baked beans

Serves 4

1 cup (250ml) dry white wine
2 cups (500ml) tomato puree
1 cup (250ml) good-quality barbecue sauce*
2 tbs brown sugar
1 tbs molasses
1 tbs Dijon mustard
2 x 400g cans cannellini beans, rinsed, drained
1 Toulouse sausage* or 12 thin pork sausages
Rocket leaves, to serve

Combine the wine, tomato puree, barbecue sauce, sugar, molasses and mustard in a saucepan over medium-low heat and simmer, stirring occasionally, for 6-8 minutes until reduced by half. Add the beans to the sauce and cook for a further 10 minutes until the mixture thickens.

Meanwhile, heat a lightly oiled chargrill pan, frypan or barbecue on medium heat and cook the Toulouse sausage for 5-6 minutes each side until cooked through. (Or cook the thin pork sausages, in batches, for 8-10 minutes until browned and cooked through.)

Cut the Toulouse sausage into 4 pieces, then serve with the baked beans and rocket leaves.

* Good-quality barbecue sauce is from gourmet food shops and delis. Toulouse sausage is a long, coiled French pork sausage, available from selected butchers.

vineyard sausages

Serves 4

1 tbs extra virgin olive oil, plus extra to drizzle
12 pork chipolatas (or use 4 chicken or pork sausages)
1 eschalot, finely chopped
2 cups (350g) mixed seedless grapes
1/2 cup (125ml) dry white wine
2 tsp chopped rosemary leaves
2 tsp honey
Grilled bread and chopped chives, to serve

Heat the olive oil in a frypan over medium-high heat. Add the
sausages and cook, turning, for 8-10 minutes until cooked
through and golden. Remove the sausages to a plate, cover
with foil and keep warm.

Drain any excess fat from the frypan, then return the pan to
medium heat. Add the eschalot and grapes and cook, stirring,
for 3-4 minutes until the grapes start to soften and begin to
lose their juice. Add the wine, rosemary and honey, then stir
for a further minute until heated through. Serve the sausages
and grape mixture over grilled bread, drizzled with extra oil
and sprinkled with chives.

tomato soup with spaghetti and chicken meatballs

Serves 4-6

1 tbs olive oil
1 onion, thinly sliced
2 garlic cloves, finely chopped
1 tbs tomato paste
2 x 400g cans chopped tomatoes
1.25L (5 cups) chicken stock
500g thin chicken sausages
100g spaghetti, broken into 5cm lengths
Chopped basil, grated parmesan and crusty bread, to serve

Heat the oil in a large saucepan over medium heat. Add the onion and cook for 2-3 minutes, stirring, until softened. Add the garlic and tomato paste and cook, stirring, for a further 1 minute. Add the tomatoes and $2^{1}/_{2}$ cups (625ml) of the chicken stock. Bring to the boil, then reduce the heat to low and simmer for 20 minutes while you make the meatballs.

For the meatballs, place the remaining $2^{1}/_{2}$ cups (625ml) chicken stock in a saucepan and bring to the boil. Squeeze the sausage meat from the casings and form into about 30 small (3cm) meatballs. Add meatballs to the stock and simmer for 10 minutes until cooked through. Remove meatballs to a plate with a slotted spoon, then return stock to the boil. Add the spaghetti and cook until al dente. Drain, discarding the stock.

Use a stick blender to blend the soup until smooth (or blend in batches in a blender, then return to the pan). Add the cooked spaghetti and meatballs to the soup and warm through gently for 5 minutes over low heat. Ladle the soup into bowls, garnish with basil and parmesan, then serve with bread.

frankfurts with stir-fried red cabbage

Serves 4

8 good-quality Continental frankfurts
1 tbs sunflower oil
30g unsalted butter
1 red onion, thinly sliced
1 green apple, peeled, sliced
1 garlic clove, chopped
400g red cabbage, thinly sliced
2 tbs red wine vinegar
2 tbs apple and sage jelly* or redcurrant jelly
1 tbs chopped flat-leaf parsley
Rye bread (optional), to serve

Heat a chargrill pan or frypan over medium heat and cook frankfurts for 2-3 minutes, turning, until heated through. (Or simmer in a saucepan of boiling water for 3-4 minutes.)

Heat oil and butter in a wok or deep frypan over medium heat. Add onion, apple and garlic and stir-fry for 2-3 minutes until onion just softens. Add the cabbage and stir-fry for 2-3 minutes until wilted. Stir in the vinegar, jelly and parsley, then season and heat through. Transfer to a platter or large serving dish and toss with the frankfurts. Serve with rye bread, if desired.
* Sage and apple jelly is from gourmet food shops (see Glossary).

pepper steak burger

Serves 4

800g beef mince
1 onion, finely chopped
1 egg, lightly beaten
¼ cup chopped flat-leaf parsley leaves
1 tbs olive oil
2 tbs green peppercorns in brine, drained,
　　lightly crushed with a fork
2 tbs brandy
1 tsp Dijon mustard
150ml thickened cream
4 slices sourdough, chargrilled,
　　rubbed with a halved garlic clove

Preheat the oven to 170°C.

Place beef, onion, egg and 2 tablespoons parsley in a bowl, season, then mix well with your hands. Using damp hands, form into 4 thick patties. Cover and chill for 10 minutes.

Heat the oil in a frypan over medium heat. Cook the patties for 2 minutes each side until sealed. Transfer to a baking tray, then bake for 5 minutes or until cooked through.

Meanwhile, drain the excess fat from the pan. Add the peppercorns, brandy, mustard and cream to the pan, then simmer over medium-low heat, stirring, for 2-3 minutes until slightly thickened. Season with sea salt, then stir in the remaining tablespoon chopped parsley.

Place a piece of grilled sourdough on each plate, top with burger patties, drizzle with the pepper sauce and serve.

prawn burgers

Serves 4

$1/2$ cup (150g) whole-egg mayonnaise
1 tbs capers, rinsed, drained
2 tsp wholegrain mustard
1 tbs chopped dill, plus extra to garnish
4 panini or hamburger buns, split
Butter lettuce leaves and
   thinly sliced red onion, to serve
1 avocado, sliced
16 cooked prawns (about 500g),
   peeled, deveined

Combine the mayonnaise, capers, mustard and dill in
a bowl, then season with salt and pepper and set aside.
   Grill or toast the buns. Spread both sides with the caper
mayonnaise, then fill with lettuce leaves, sliced avocado,
prawns, onion and extra dill.

smoked trout burgers with asparagus tzatziki

Serves 4

1 bunch asparagus, woody ends trimmed
1 egg
2 x 170g skinless hot-smoked ocean trout portions*
1¼ cups (85g) fresh wholemeal breadcrumbs
Grated zest and juice of 1 lemon
2 tbs chopped mint leaves
200g thick Greek-style yoghurt
2 garlic cloves, crushed
2 tbs olive oil
4 wholemeal rolls or hamburger buns, split, toasted
Watercress sprigs and lemon wedges, to serve

Cook asparagus in boiling salted water for 2 minutes, then drain and refresh in cold water. Remove and reserve the tips. Chop the stalks, then place in a food processor with the egg. Blend until well combined. Add trout, breadcrumbs, lemon zest and juice, and half the mint and pulse to combine. Season to taste with salt and pepper. Using damp hands, form the mixture into 4 patties. Cover and chill for 30 minutes.

Shred the asparagus tips using a sharp knife, then fold into the yoghurt with the garlic and remaining mint. Season well, then cover and chill the asparagus tzatziki until required.

Heat the oil in a frypan over medium-high heat. Cook the trout patties for 2 minutes each side or until golden brown. Fill the toasted buns with tzatziki, patties and watercress, then serve with lemon wedges.

* Available from supermarkets and delis.

pork, sage & onion burgers

Serves 4

450g pork sausages
1/2 packet (100g) sage and onion stuffing mix*
1 egg
Olive oil, to brush
4 Turkish rolls or panini, split, toasted
Baby spinach or rocket leaves, cranberry
    sauce and sour cream, to serve

Remove the sausage casings, then place the sausage meat
in a bowl with the stuffing and egg, season, then mix well with
your hands. Using damp hands, form the mixture into 4 patties.
Cover and chill for 30 minutes.
   Preheat the oven to 170°C. Brush a frypan or chargrill pan
with oil and heat over medium-high heat. Cook the patties for
2-3 minutes each side until golden. Transfer to a tray, then bake
for 5-6 minutes until cooked through. Fill toasted rolls with
spinach, patties, cranberry sauce and sour cream.
* Stuffing mix is available from supermarkets (see Glossary).

meatball sliders

Serves 4-6 (makes 12)

'Sliders', or mini burgers, are very popular in the US. This Italian meatball version is so good, you won't be able to stop at one.

200g each beef, pork and veal mince
$1/2$ cup (35g) fresh breadcrumbs
$2/3$ cup (50g) grated pecorino cheese
   or parmesan, plus extra to serve
1 egg, plus 1 extra yolk
2 tbs chopped flat-leaf parsley leaves
2 tbs olive oil
700ml jar tomato passata (sugo)*
12 small bread rolls, split
2 cups wild rocket leaves

Use your hands to mix the beef, pork and veal mince, breadcrumbs, cheese, egg, egg yolk and parsley together in a bowl, then season with salt and pepper. Using damp hands, form heaped tablespoons of the mixture into 12 large meatballs. Cover and chill for 20 minutes.

Heat the oil in a large ovenproof frypan over medium-high heat. Fry the meatballs, in batches, for 3-4 minutes, turning, until golden all over. Remove meatballs and set aside.

Carefully drain excess oil from the pan. Add the passata to the pan, then simmer over low heat for 5 minutes. Return the meatballs to the pan and simmer for a further 5-6 minutes until cooked through and the sauce thickens slightly.

Fill each roll with rocket, a meatball, sauce and extra cheese.
* Sieved tomatoes, from supermarkets and greengrocers.

asian-marinated baked salmon

Serves 4-6

This recipe comes from my dear friend Karen Thomas. She serves up this beautiful dish with big bowls of thick handcut chips – a little "out there" with an Asian-inspired dish, but that's Karen!

2 lemongrass stems (pale part only), chopped
1/2 cup (125ml) dark soy sauce
1/2 bunch coriander, leaves thinly sliced, stalks finely chopped
2cm piece ginger, finely grated
4 garlic cloves, finely grated
1kg piece skinless salmon fillet, pin-boned
   (ask your fishmonger for a whole fillet)
1/3 cup (115g) honey, warmed
4 spring onions, finely shredded
2 limes, halved
Mixed pea salad (we used fresh peas, snow peas
   and pea shoots), to serve

Bash lemongrass in a mortar with a pestle until fragrant. Stir in the soy sauce, coriander stalks, ginger and garlic. Place the salmon in a glass dish, then spread all over with the marinade. Cover and marinate in the fridge for 1 hour.

Preheat the oven to 200°C and line a large tray with baking paper. Place the salmon on the tray, then brush with the honey. Bake for 10 minutes or until the fish is just cooked but still a little pink in the centre.

Carefully transfer the fish to a board or serving platter, sprinkle with spring onion and coriander leaves, then serve warm or at room temperature with lime to squeeze and salad.

green curry with smoked salmon

Serves 4

3 kaffir lime leaves*
1 pontiac potato (about 300g), peeled,
   cut into 2cm cubes
3 tbs Thai green curry paste
300ml coconut milk
150g thin green beans, trimmed,
   cut into 4cm lengths
1 tbs fish sauce
1 tbs light soy sauce
Juice of 1 lime
2 tsp grated palm sugar* or brown sugar
4 x 175g hot-smoked salmon portions*,
   broken into large chunks
Jasmine rice, to serve

Finely shred 1 kaffir lime leaf and set aside to garnish. Par-cook
the potato in boiling salted water for 5 minutes. Drain.
   Heat a wok or deep frypan over medium heat. Add the curry
paste and stir-fry for 1 minute until fragrant. Add the coconut
milk and remaining 2 lime leaves, then bring to the boil. Add
the potato, turn the heat to low, then simmer for 5 minutes.
Add beans and cook for a further 2 minutes, then stir in the
fish sauce, soy, lime juice and sugar, adjusting to taste. Gently
stir in the salmon, then cook for a further 1-2 minutes until
the vegetables are tender and salmon is heated through.
Garnish with the shredded lime leaf, then serve with rice.
* Kaffir lime leaves and palm sugar are from Asian food shops.
Hot-smoked salmon portions are from supermarkets.

tea 'smoked' salmon

Serves 4

Smoking fish is quite a performance, and the strong smell
can hang around in the kitchen for days. This cheat's version
uses smoky black lapsang souchong tea from China for a
similar flavour without the fuss.

2 lapsang souchong teabags*
1 garlic clove, finely chopped
5cm piece ginger, grated
1/3 cup (80ml) kecap manis (Indonesian sweet soy sauce)*
1 tbs honey
1 tbs sesame oil
4 salmon fillets with skin
1 tbs olive oil
Jasmine rice and steamed Asian greens, to serve

Place the teabags in a jug, pour over 200ml boiling water, and
leave for 5 minutes to infuse. Press the teabags against the
side of the jug to extract maximum flavour, then discard. Add
the garlic, ginger, kecap manis, honey and half the sesame oil
and stir until combined, then allow to cool. Place the salmon in
a glass or ceramic dish and pour over the marinade, then cover
and marinate in the fridge for at least 4 hours or overnight.

Remove the salmon from the marinade, reserving 1/2 cup
(125ml), and pat dry with paper towel. Heat the remaining
sesame oil and olive oil in a frypan over medium-high heat
and cook the salmon, skin-side down for 2 minutes, then
turn and cook for 2 minutes (or until done to your liking).

Meanwhile, bring the reserved marinade to a gentle simmer
over medium-low heat (don't allow to boil). Serve the salmon
on rice with Asian greens, drizzled with the sauce.
* Lapsang souchong teabags are from selected supermarkets.
Kecap manis is from Asian food shops.

SALMON

salmon poached in olive oil and vanilla

Serves 4

It's a little extravagant to use a litre of olive oil for poaching, but a well-priced supermarket oil will do, and you'll be rewarded with amazing flavour thanks to the fragrant vanilla bean. You need a kitchen thermometer for this recipe.

1L (4 cups) extra virgin olive oil
1 vanilla bean, split lengthways, seeds scraped
1-2 tarragon sprigs*
2 eschalots, sliced
4 x 120g skinless salmon fillets, pinboned
Cauliflower puree or mashed potato, lemon wedges
   and baby spinach leaves, to serve

Place the olive oil, vanilla pod and seeds, tarragon and eschalot in a flameproof casserole or deep frypan (big enough to fit the salmon in a single layer) and warm gently over low heat for 3-4 minutes. Remove from the heat, then cover and stand for at least 4 hours, or overnight, for the flavours to infuse.

   Season the salmon and place in the oil mixture, ensuring the fish is completely covered. Place the pan over very low heat, bring the temperature to 100°C (use a kitchen thermometer – there should be only the slightest ripple in the oil), then poach for 15 minutes. Remove the salmon from the oil with a fish slice – it will still be very pink inside but gently cooked.

   Serve the salmon on cauliflower puree or mash with lemon wedges and spinach, drizzled with a little of the poaching oil.
* Fresh tarragon is available from selected greengrocers.

sesame salmon roulades with green papaya salad

Serves 4

250g green papaya* or green mango*
1/3 cup (80ml) lime juice
2 tbs fish sauce
2 tbs grated palm sugar*
2 small red chillies, seeds removed, finely chopped
4 x 150g skinless salmon fillets, pin-boned
1/4 cup (35g) sesame seeds
1 tbs sunflower oil, plus extra to drizzle
2 tbs chopped coriander, plus extra leaves to garnish
2 tbs chopped mint leaves, plus extra leaves to garnish
2 tbs chopped toasted peanuts, plus extra to garnish

Preheat the oven to 170°C.

Cut the papaya or mango flesh into thin matchsticks using a mandoline or coarsely grate. Place in a large bowl. Shake the lime juice, fish sauce, sugar and chilli in a screw-top jar, then toss with the papaya or mango. Set aside.

Slice each salmon fillet horizontally through the centre, leaving 1 end intact, then open out into a long strip. Turn each fillet over and season, then tightly roll and secure each one on a skewer. Place the sesame seeds in a dish, dip in the roulades to coat on both sides, then drizzle with extra oil.

Heat the oil in a non-stick ovenproof frypan over medium heat and sear the roulades for 1 minute each side to lightly toast the seeds. Transfer the pan to the oven for 5 minutes until the fish is just cooked.

Meanwhile, toss the herbs and nuts with the salad. Serve the salmon on the salad, garnished with extra herbs and peanuts.

* Available from Asian food shops and selected greengrocers.

cajun fish with corn & avocado salsa

Serves 4

2 tbs brown sugar
1/2 tsp each of chilli powder, ground cumin,
   paprika and mustard powder
4 skinless thick white fish fillets
   (such as blue-eye or coral trout)
1 tbs olive oil, plus extra to brush
Light sour cream, loosened with enough warm water
   to form a pouring consistency, to serve

Corn & avocado salsa
1 avocado, finely chopped
400g can corn kernels, drained
250g tomatoes, seeds removed, finely chopped
1 red onion, finely chopped
1 tsp sesame oil
2 tbs olive oil
1 cup chopped coriander leaves
Juice of 1 lime

Preheat the oven to 180°C.
   Combine the sugar, chilli, cumin, paprika, mustard powder,
1 teaspoon pepper and 1/2 teaspoon salt in a shallow bowl. Brush
the fish with extra olive oil, then coat well in the spice mixture.
   Heat the oil in a large ovenproof frypan over medium heat.
Add the fish and cook for 2-3 minutes each side until golden.
Transfer to the oven for 5 minutes or until just cooked.
   Meanwhile, for the salsa, combine all the ingredients in
a bowl and season to taste. Serve the fish topped with the
salsa and drizzled with the sour cream.

whole fish with roast capsicum & chilli butter

Serves 4

4 small (about 350g each) whole fish
  (such as lemon sole or small snapper)
2 tbs olive oil, plus extra to brush
1 roasted red capsicum
  (or a 280g jar chargrilled capsicum*, drained)
100g unsalted butter
Finely grated zest of 1 lemon, plus 1 tbs lemon juice
2 tbs finely chopped coriander leaves
1 small red chilli, seeds removed, finely chopped
1 garlic clove, finely chopped

Preheat the oven to 200°C. Lightly grease 2 baking trays.

Cut 3 slashes in the thickest part of each fish on one side. Place 2 fish, cut-side up, on each tray, then brush with the extra oil and season with salt and pepper. Bake for 10-12 minutes until the fish is cooked (it will flake easily away from the bone).

Meanwhile, very finely chop the capsicum, then place in a small saucepan with the olive oil, butter, lemon zest and juice, coriander, chilli and garlic. Season. Stir over low heat until butter is melted and well combined. Keep warm.

Serve the fish drizzled with the capsicum & chilli butter.

* Available from supermarkets and delis (see Glossary)

pan-fried fish with malt-vinegar tartare

Serves 4

Fish and chips with malt vinegar was a regular Friday-night dinner when I was growing up in England. I love its rich caramel flavour, but if you prefer you can use white wine vinegar instead.

2 tbs olive oil
8 boneless white fish fillets with skin (such as coral trout)
1/2 cup (150g) whole-egg mayonnaise
3 tbs thickened cream
1/3 cup (80ml) malt vinegar, plus extra to serve
1 tbs finely chopped cornichons (small pickled cucumbers)
1 tbs chopped fresh tarragon leaves*
1 tbs finely chopped flat-leaf parsley,
    plus extra to garnish
Oven-baked chips, to serve

Heat the oil in a large non-stick frypan over medium heat. Season the fish, add to the pan and cook for 2 minutes each side or until the skin is crispy and fish is cooked through. Set aside in a warm place while you make the sauce.
   Drain most of the oil from the pan. Add the mayonnaise, cream, vinegar and cornichon, and stir for 1-2 minutes to warm through. Remove from the heat, then stir in the tarragon and parsley.
   Divide the fish and chips among plates, then drizzle with the tartare sauce. Season with salt and pepper, garnish with parsley, and serve with extra malt vinegar for the chips.
* Fresh tarragon is from selected greengrocers.

tandoori swordfish with lemon achar

Serves 4

3 tbs (75g) tandoori paste
3 tbs (70g) thick Greek-style yoghurt
4 x 180g swordfish steaks
1 tbs vegetable oil
2 tsp black mustard seeds
3 preserved lemon quarters*, white pith
   and flesh removed, rind thinly sliced
1 long red chilli, seeds removed, thinly sliced
1 tsp ground turmeric
12 fresh curry leaves*
1 tbs white wine vinegar
2 tsp caster sugar
2 tomatoes, seeds removed, sliced
Fried pappadams and steamed basmati rice, to serve

Combine the tandoori paste and yoghurt in a shallow dish.
Add the swordfish steaks and turn to coat in the mixture,
then cover and marinate in the fridge for 1 hour.

Meanwhile, for the lemon achar, heat the oil in a frypan over
medium heat. Add mustard seeds and cook for 1 minute or
until they start to pop. Add the preserved lemon, chilli, turmeric
and curry leaves and cook, stirring, for 3 minutes. Combine the
vinegar and sugar in a small bowl, stirring to dissolve the sugar,
then add to the pan with the tomato. Stir to combine, then
remove from the heat and set aside to cool.

Preheat a chargrill pan or barbecue on medium-high,
then cook the fish for 2 minutes each side or until cooked
but still moist in the centre. Serve the swordfish with the
achar, pappadams and rice.

* Preserved lemons are from gourmet shops and delis. Fresh
curry leaves are from selected greengrocers and Asian shops.

fish tagine

Serves 4

Meat-based tagines are all about long, slow cooking, but this
seafood version is the fast route to Moroccan flavours. To make
it even quicker, use a good marinara mix from your fishmonger.

2 tbs olive oil
1 large red onion, thinly sliced
2 tbs chermoula paste*
400g can chopped tomatoes
1 cinnamon quill
600g mixed fish and seafood (we used red mullet fillets,
    ling pieces and prawns)
1/2 cup green olives
1 tbs chopped coriander
Couscous and flatbread, to serve

Heat the oil in a large heavy-based saucepan over medium
heat. Add the onion and cook for 2 minutes until softened.
Add the chermoula and stir for a few seconds until fragrant,
then add the tomato, cinnamon and 350ml water. Bring to
the boil, then reduce heat to medium-low and simmer for
10 minutes until thickened. Add the seafood and simmer
for a further 8-10 minutes until just cooked. Remove from
the heat, stir in the olives and sprinkle with coriander.
Serve with couscous and flatbread.
* Chermoula is a North African herb and spice paste,
from Middle Eastern and gourmet shops (see Glossary).

spicy garlic prawns cooked in beer

Serves 4

This would have to be every man's died-and-gone-to-heaven dish. The idea is to suck the sweet meat from the prawn shell, then wash it all down with plenty more cold beer.

1kg green king prawns
80g unsalted butter
½ tsp smoked paprika* (pimenton)
4 garlic cloves, finely chopped
Pinch of peri peri spice mix* or ½ tsp Tabasco (to taste)
¾ cup (185ml) lager
2 tbs chopped flat-leaf parsley
Shoestring fries, to serve

Halve prawns by splitting lengthways through the middle with a sharp knife. Remove vein, rinse, then pat dry with paper towel.

Melt 40g butter in a large frypan over medium-high heat. When sizzling, cook the prawns, in 2 batches, for 1 minute each side, then remove from the pan and set aside.

Melt the remaining 40g butter in the pan with the paprika, garlic and peri peri or Tabasco. Cook, stirring, for 1 minute until fragrant. Add the beer, increase the heat to high and cook for 2-3 minutes until the sauce thickens slightly. Remove from the heat, add the prawns and parsley and toss to combine. Serve the prawns with shoestring fries and cold beer.
* Smoked paprika and peri peri spice mix (see Glossary) are available from gourmet food shops and delis.

prawn, chilli & pesto pizza

Makes 2 pizzas

10 green prawns, peeled, deveined, chopped
2 tbs olive oil
2 garlic cloves, crushed
1/4 tsp dried chilli flakes
2 woodfired pizza bases*
1/3 cup good-quality tomato pasta sauce
   or tomato passata (sugo)*
100g shredded mozzarella or pizza cheese*
10 cherry tomatoes, halved
2 tbs basil pesto, to serve

Place the prawn meat in a bowl with the olive oil, garlic and
chilli. Toss to combine, then set aside.
   Preheat the oven to 220°C (or heat a pizza maker on 2¹/₂).
Spread the bases with the pizza sauce and scatter with cheese.
Arrange the tomato, cut-side up, over the base, then scatter
over the prawn mixture, including the oil.
   Cook the pizzas for 6 minutes or until the prawns are
just cooked, the cheese is bubbling and the bases are crisp.
Serve drizzled with pesto.
* Available from supermarkets and delis.

scallops with peperonata and aioli

Serves 4

290g jar peperonata*
2 tbs tomato passata (sugo)*
20 scallops without roe
2 tbs olive oil
50g mixed baby salad leaves (mesclun)
200g jar aioli (garlic mayonnaise)*
Extra virgin olive oil, to drizzle

Warm the peperonata and passata in a saucepan over low heat for 2-3 minutes until heated through. Season with salt and pepper.

Brush both sides of the scallops with the oil, then season. Heat a large frypan over high heat and cook the scallops, in batches, for 30 seconds each side until golden brown but still translucent in the centre.

Divide the peperonata mixture, scallops and salad leaves among serving plates. Season with salt and pepper, drizzle the plate with extra virgin olive oil, then serve with aioli.

* Peperonata (see Glossary), passata and aioli are available from supermarkets and delis.

prawn cocktails

Serves 4

Mascarpone cheese adds a perfect richness to this classic Marie Rose cocktail sauce.

2 tbs tomato sauce (ketchup)
$2/3$ cup (200g) mayonnaise
3 tbs (65g) mascarpone cheese
Lemon juice and Tabasco, to taste
400g cooked prawns, peeled,
   deveined, cut into chunks
$1/2$ telegraph cucumber,
   thinly sliced on an angle
$1/4$ iceberg lettuce, cut into thin wedges
Paprika, to dust

Combine the tomato sauce, mayonnaise and mascarpone in a bowl. Add lemon juice and Tabasco to taste, then season with salt and pepper. Add the prawn meat and stir to coat in the mayonnaise mixture.

Arrange the cucumber slices and lettuce wedges in 4 martini glasses or glass serving bowls. Pile the prawn mixture on top of the lettuce, then serve sprinkled with a little paprika.

spanish mussels with chorizo

Serves 4

This is a one-pot-wonder that you can just pop on the table and serve with lots of crusty bread to mop up the sauce.

2 tbs olive oil
1 onion, sliced
1 chorizo sausage, peeled, chopped
1 tsp smoked paprika* (pimenton)
3 garlic cloves, finely chopped
1/4 tsp saffron threads
400g can chopped tomatoes
3/4 cup (185ml) dry sherry
2kg (about 36) black mussels, scrubbed, debearded
1/4 cup flat-leaf parsley leaves, torn
Crusty bread, to serve

Heat the oil in a large flameproof casserole or lidded deep frypan over medium-high heat. Add the onion, chorizo and 1 teaspoon salt and cook, stirring, for 2-3 minutes until onion is soft. Add the paprika, garlic and saffron and stir to combine. Add tomato and sherry and simmer for 3 minutes. Add the mussels, cover and cook for 3 minutes, shaking the pan from time to time, until the mussels open (discard any mussels that haven't opened after this time). Scatter with the parsley and serve with bread to dip into the sauce.
* From gourmet food shops and delis.

goat's cheese, roast capsicum & spinach lasagne

Serves 4-6

400g baby spinach leaves
200ml creme fraiche or light sour cream
100ml pure (thin) cream
2 eggs, beaten
$1/2$ cup (40g) grated parmesan
750g roast capsicum pieces*
250g soft goat's cheese
375g fresh lasagne sheets
Green salad, to serve

Preheat the oven to 190°C. Blanch the spinach for 1 minute in boiling water until wilted. Drain in a sieve, pressing down to remove excess liquid. Cool.

Combine creme fraiche, cream, eggs and half the parmesan in a bowl. Season with salt and pepper.

Pat the roast capsicum with paper towel to remove excess oil. Spread a third of the cream mixture over the base of a 20cm x 26cm (1.5-litre) baking dish, cover with half the capsicum, crumble over half the goat's cheese, then layer with half the spinach. Cover with pasta sheets, cutting to fit. Repeat the layers, then finish with a final layer of cream mixture. Sprinkle with remaining parmesan, then cover with baking paper and foil.

Bake for 30 minutes, then remove the paper and foil and bake for a further 10-15 minutes until the top is golden and bubbling. Stand for 5 minutes, then slice and serve with a green salad.

* Available from supermarkets and delis.

moroccan carrot & chickpea stew

Serves 4

2 tbs olive oil
1 onion, thinly sliced
3 garlic cloves, finely chopped
1/2 tsp each ground coriander, cumin,
    turmeric, ginger, cayenne and paprika
2 bunches baby (Dutch) carrots, peeled,
    ends trimmed with some stem left intact
1 parsnip, peeled, cut into batons
400g can chopped tomatoes
2 tbs lemon juice
1 cup (250ml) vegetable stock or water
400g can chickpeas, drained, rinsed
1/3 cup chopped coriander leaves
2 tsp chopped mint leaves
Couscous, to serve

Heat the oil in a large saucepan over medium heat. Add the onion and cook, stirring, for 2 minutes or until starting to soften. Add the garlic and spices and stir for a few seconds until fragrant, then add the carrots and parsnip and stir to coat in the spices. Stir in the tomato, lemon juice and stock or water, then cover and simmer for about 20 minutes or until the vegetables are tender. Add the chickpeas and heat through for 2-3 minutes. Remove from the heat, then stir through the coriander and mint. Serve with couscous.

VEGETARIAN

vegetable terrine with tarragon and basil

Serves 6-8

1 carrot, cut into 1cm cubes
1 potato, peeled, cut into 1cm cubes
100g fresh or frozen broad beans
100g thin green beans, cut into 1cm lengths
100g fresh or frozen baby peas
6 eggs, lightly beaten
300ml thickened cream
1 tbs each chopped fresh tarragon* and basil leaves
Tomato chutney and salad leaves, to serve

Preheat oven to 180°C. Lightly grease a 1-litre terrine or loaf pan.
  Cook the carrot and potato in a pan of boiling salted water for 2-3 minutes until just tender. Remove to a bowl with a slotted spoon. Return water to the boil, then add broad and green beans. Blanch for 1-2 minutes until thin beans are bright green. Drain, then slip the broad beans out of their tough skins and toss all the vegetables together in the bowl. Allow to cool.
  Whisk the eggs and cream together in a separate bowl.
  Pack a layer of vegetables in the terrine, then sprinkle with some of the herbs and season well. Carefully pour over enough egg mixture to cover, then repeat the process with remaining vegetables, herbs and egg mixture (this will help ensure the vegetables are evenly distributed). Cover with a sheet of baking paper cut to fit, then cover tightly with foil. Place the terrine in a roasting pan and fill with enough boiling water to come halfway up the sides of the terrine. Bake for 50 minutes or until a skewer inserted in the centre comes out clean. Remove the terrine from the water bath and cool completely. Chill for 1 hour to firm up, then bring back to room temperature before serving. Turn out and cut into 2cm-thick slices, then serve with chutney and salad.
* Fresh tarragon is available from selected greengrocers.

stuffed field mushrooms with pesto

Serves 4

6 slices sourdough bread, crusts removed
2/3 cup (180g) basil pesto
8 field mushrooms or large Swiss brown mushrooms,
    stalks trimmed
1/3 cup (80ml) olive oil
4 sprigs cherry truss tomatoes
2 tbs vino cotto* or balsamic vinegar

Preheat the oven to 180°C. Grease a large baking tray.
    Place the bread in a food processor and process until you
have fine breadcrumbs. Add the pesto, season with salt and
pepper, then process to combine.
    Place the mushrooms, cap-side down, on the tray and brush
with half the olive oil. Season, then fill each mushroom with
some of the breadcrumb mixture. Arrange the tomatoes around
the mushrooms, drizzle with the remaining olive oil, then
season with salt and pepper.
    Bake for 8-10 minutes until the tomatoes start to collapse and
the mushrooms are tender. Drizzle with the vino cotto, then swirl
the pan around to combine the vino cotto with any pan juices.
Serve the mushrooms and tomatoes drizzled with the juices.
* Vino cotto (also known as saba) is available from Italian delis
and gourmet food shops.

pumpkin, goat's cheese & onion marmalade jalousie

Serves 4-6

700g pumpkin, peeled, cut into 2cm pieces
1 tbs olive oil
1 tbs chopped rosemary leaves
2 x 375g blocks frozen puff pastry, thawed
375g jar onion marmalade*
150g soft goat's cheese
1 egg, beaten

Preheat the oven to 200°C.

Spread the pumpkin on a lined baking tray and toss with the olive oil, salt and pepper. Sprinkle with rosemary and roast for 30 minutes or until tender. Cool.

Reduce the oven to 180°C. Roll out 1 block of pastry on a lightly floured surface to form a 20cm x 30cm rectangle. Place on a lined tray and prick the base in several places with a fork, leaving a 2cm border. Spread the base inside the border with two-thirds of the onion marmalade, then top with the pumpkin and goat's cheese. Season with salt and pepper. Brush the pastry border with egg.

Roll out the second block of pastry slightly larger than the first. Fold the pastry in half lengthways and use a sharp knife to make cuts in the folded side, about 1cm apart and leaving a 2cm border on the unfolded side. Carefully open the pastry back out and place over the filling, pressing to seal the edges – the cuts in the pastry should separate slightly to reveal some of the filling. Trim the edges if necessary, then brush all over with beaten egg. Bake for 30 minutes or until puffed and golden, then serve with the remaining onion marmalade.

* Available from delis and gourmet food shops.

roast pumpkin &
white bean salad

Serves 4

This salad is perfect as a vegetarian main course
or served with grilled meat, especially lamb.

1kg butternut pumpkin, peeled, cut into 2cm cubes
100ml olive oil, plus extra to drizzle
1 tbs soy sauce
1 long red chilli, seeds removed, chopped
2 tsp honey
1 garlic clove, finely chopped
400g can cannellini beans, rinsed, drained
2 cups wild rocket
1 cup coriander leaves

Preheat the oven to 180°C. Line a baking tray with baking paper.
   Place the pumpkin on the baking tray, drizzle with a little extra
olive oil and season with sea salt and freshly ground black pepper.
Roast, turning once or twice, for 25 minutes or until pumpkin is
golden and tender. Allow to cool slightly.
   Whisk the 100ml olive oil, soy sauce, chilli, honey and garlic
together in a large bowl. Add the beans, rocket, coriander and
pumpkin. Toss well to coat in the dressing, then serve.

mulled-wine pear & goat's cheese salad

Serves 4

2 cups (500ml) dry red wine
1/2 cup (110g) caster sugar
1 cinnamon quill
2 star anise
4 small sensation or corella pears, peeled, halved, cored
Bunch of watercress, sprigs picked
1/3 cup (50g) hazelnuts, toasted, roughly chopped
1 cup croutons
1/4 cup (60ml) olive oil
1 tbs red wine vinegar
2 x 150g ash-covered goat's cheese logs*, sliced into rounds

Place the red wine, sugar, cinnamon and star anise in a
saucepan over low heat. Stir to dissolve the sugar, then add
the pears and poach gently over low heat for 8-10 minutes
until tender (this will depend on the ripeness of the pears).
Leave to cool completely in the liquid.

Combine the watercress, hazelnuts and croutons in a large
bowl. In a separate bowl, whisk the olive oil and red wine
vinegar together with 1 tablespoon of the poaching liquid.
Season well with salt and pepper. Divide the salad among
4 serving plates, top each with 2 pear halves and some
goat's cheese slices, then serve drizzled with the dressing.
* From delis and selected supermarkets.

prawn, risoni & feta salad

Serves 6-8

1⅓ cups (300g) risoni pasta (orzo)
1 telegraph cucumber, peeled, seeds removed, chopped
1 bunch watercress, leaves picked
1 cup roughly chopped flat-leaf parsley
1 fennel bulb, halved, very thinly sliced
  (a mandoline is ideal for this)
800g cooked prawns, peeled (tails intact)
1 preserved lemon quarter*, white pith and flesh discarded,
  rind finely chopped, plus 1 tbs preserving liquid
1 cup (120g) pitted green olives, sliced
150g feta cheese
2 tbs lemon juice
¼ cup (60ml) extra virgin olive oil

Cook the pasta in boiling salted water according to packet
instructions. Rinse in cold water and drain, then place in a large
bowl with the cucumber, watercress, parsley, fennel, prawns,
lemon rind and olives. Crumble in the feta.

Whisk the preserved lemon liquid with the lemon juice and
oil, then season to taste with salt and pepper. Add to the salad
and toss gently to combine, then serve.

* Preserved lemon is from delis and Middle Eastern shops.

the best green salad with white wine dressing

Serves 4-6

It makes me laugh when I order a green salad in a restaurant and it comes with tomato, onions and olives! This is the definitive green salad, and a dressing with a twist.

1 small frisee lettuce (curly endive)
2 baby cos lettuces
2 cups wild rocket leaves
1 handful chervil sprigs*
2 handfuls baby green beans, blanched for
    1-2 minutes in boiling water
Bunch of chives
$^1/_3$ cup (80ml) white wine
$^1/_4$ cup (60ml) lemon juice
1 tsp honey
$^3/_4$ cup (185ml) extra virgin olive oil

Remove the outer leaves from the frisee and cos. Wash the inner leaves with the rocket, then spin in a salad spinner or pat dry with paper towel. Pick the chervil leaves and place in a serving bowl with the lettuce and beans. Hold the bunch of chives over the bowl and use kitchen scissors to finely snip half the bunch into the bowl.

In a separate bowl, whisk the wine, lemon juice and honey and season with salt and pepper. Slowly whisk in the oil until you have an emulsified dressing. Toss the salad and dressing together, then garnish with remaining chives and serve.
* Chervil is available from selected greengrocers.

heirloom tomato salad with cheat's burrata

Serves 6

Burrata is an Italian fresh mozzarella filled with cream, which oozes out onto the plate when you tear it open. It's hard to find here in Australia, but this makes a great alternative.

3 buffalo mozzarella balls* (about 750g total), drained
2 garlic cloves, finely chopped
200ml creme fraiche
200ml thickened cream
1.2kg assorted heirloom tomatoes* (such as Black Russian and Tigerella), or use vine-ripened tomatoes
2 loosely packed cups basil leaves
Extra virgin olive oil, to drizzle

Tear the mozzarella into large pieces. Toss in a bowl with the garlic, creme fraiche and cream, then season with sea salt and freshly ground black pepper. Set aside.

Slice the tomatoes and arrange on a platter or in a shallow serving bowl. Season and scatter with the basil leaves. Dot the mozzarella mixture over the salad and serve drizzled with extra virgin olive oil.

* Buffalo mozzarella is available from delis and gourmet food shops. Heirloom tomatoes are available from selected greengrocers and growers' markets.

spaghetti carbonara

Serves 4

For a super-creamy sauce, sit an extra egg yolk in its shell on each dish, for your guests to stir through the pasta at the table.

1 tbs olive oil
20g unsalted butter
100g sliced pancetta, cut into thin strips
2 garlic cloves, finely chopped
400g spaghetti
3 eggs
150ml pure (thin) cream
$^2/_3$ cup (50g) grated parmesan
$^2/_3$ cup (50g) grated pecorino cheese
2 tbs chopped flat-leaf parsley

Heat the oil and butter in a frypan over medium-high heat. Add the pancetta and cook, stirring, for 3-4 minutes until starting to crisp. Stir in garlic, then remove from the heat and set aside.

Cook the pasta in a large saucepan of boiling salted water according to packet instructions. Meanwhile, beat the eggs and cream together in a bowl, then season with salt and pepper.

Drain the pasta, reserving $^1/_2$ cup (125ml) of the cooking water, then return to the saucepan off the heat. Quickly add the egg and pancetta mixtures and toss to coat the pasta. Add half each of the parmesan, pecorino and parsley, then toss to combine (the residual heat from the pasta will cook the egg.)

Divide the pasta among warm bowls, then serve topped with the remaining cheese and parsley.

mushroom &
taleggio ravioli

Serves 4 (makes 20)

Wonton wrappers are the perfect cheat's solution for fresh
pasta dishes. They're available from selected supermarkets
and Asian food shops.

2 tbs extra virgin olive oil, plus extra to drizzle
1 garlic clove, finely chopped
250g Swiss brown mushrooms, chopped
2 tbs dry Marsala (Italian fortified wine)
40 egg wonton wrappers
200g Taleggio cheese*, cut into 20 pieces
5 thin prosciutto slices, each cut into 4 small squares
Truffle oil*, small basil leaves and grated parmesan, to serve

Heat the oil in a frypan over medium heat. Add garlic and
cook, stirring, for 30 seconds. Add mushrooms, season with
salt and pepper, then cook, stirring, for 2-3 minutes until
softened and any liquid has evaporated. Stir in the Marsala,
then remove from the heat.

Lay a wonton wrapper on a work surface, then top with
a piece of cheese, a teaspoonful of the mushroom mixture
and a piece of prosciutto. Brush the edges of the wrapper with
a little water, then top with another wrapper and press down
to seal. Trim edges, then repeat with remaining wrappers and
filling to make 20 ravioli.

Bring a large saucepan of salted water to the boil. Add the
ravioli and cook for 3-4 minutes until they rise to the surface.
Remove to a plate with a slotted spoon.

Divide the ravioli among 4 plates and drizzle with olive and
truffle oils. Season with salt and pepper, then serve scattered
with basil and parmesan.

* Taleggio (an Italian washed-rind cheese) and truffle oil are
from delis and gourmet food shops.

greek-style pasta bake with lamb

Serves 3-4

This makes a perfect roast for two, with leftovers for the next day.
I like to serve this dish with a salad of crumbled feta, kalamata
olives and parsley, dressed with olive oil and a squeeze of lemon.

1 tbs olive oil
1 lamb mini roast or half leg (about 800g)
125g sliced pancetta, cut into strips
1 tbs chopped rosemary
150ml dry red wine
600ml tomato passata* (sugo)
600ml lamb* or chicken stock
1 tsp sugar
400g penne
280g jar marinated artichokes, drained, chopped
Lemon wedges, to serve

Preheat the oven to 180°C.
   Heat the oil in a large frypan over medium heat. Season
the lamb all over with salt and pepper, then add to the pan
and cook, turning, for 5 minutes or until browned. Remove
and set aside. Add the pancetta and rosemary to the pan and
cook, stirring, for 4-5 minutes until the pancetta starts to crisp.
Add the wine and bring to the boil, then add the passata, stock
and sugar. Season to taste, then pour the tomato mixture into
a roasting pan and stir in the penne.
   Set a rack over the roasting pan, then place the lamb on the
rack. Bake the lamb and pasta for 40 minutes or until the lamb
juices run clear when pierced with a skewer and the pasta is al
dente. Set the lamb aside in a warm place to rest for 10 minutes
and stir the artichoke through the pasta.
   Slice the lamb and serve with the pasta and lemon to squeeze.
* Passata (sieved tomatoes) is available in bottles from
supermarkets. Lamb stock is available from butchers.

spicy squid spaghetti

Serves 4

1 tbs extra virgin olive oil
3 garlic cloves, finely chopped
1/3 cup (80ml) dry red wine
400g can chopped tomatoes
2 tbs harissa* (or to taste)
500g fresh baby squid, cleaned, hoods lightly scored
400g spaghetti or other long thin pasta
2 tbs chopped flat-leaf parsley leaves

Heat the oil in a frypan over medium heat. Add the garlic and cook, stirring, for 1-2 minutes until softened. Add the wine, tomato and harissa and cook, stirring occasionally, for 1-2 minutes. Add the squid and season to taste. Reduce heat to low and simmer for 30-40 minutes until squid is tender, adding a little water if the sauce becomes too thick.

   Meanwhile, cook the spaghetti in a large saucepan of boiling salted water according to packet instructions. Drain the pasta and divide among bowls, then top with the squid mixture and garnish with parsley.
* Harissa is a North African chilli paste from delis and Middle Eastern food shops (see Glossary).

PASTA

macaroni cheese with truffle oil

Serves 4

400g macaroni
2-3 tbs truffle oil* (to taste), plus extra to serve
1 tbs olive oil
2 eschalots, finely chopped
4 bacon rashers, finely chopped
2 garlic cloves, finely chopped
1 tsp fresh thyme leaves
1$^{1}/_{2}$ cups (375ml) thickened cream
3 cups (360g) grated good-quality cheddar
$^{1}/_{3}$ cup (25g) grated parmesan
Grilled bread and chopped parsley, to serve

Preheat oven to 180°C and grease a 1-litre (4-cup) baking dish.

Cook the pasta in a large pan of boiling salted water according to packet instructions. Drain, then return to the pan, toss with truffle oil to taste and season.

Meanwhile, heat the olive oil in a large, deep frypan over medium heat. Add the eschalot, bacon and garlic and cook, stirring, for 2-3 minutes until the eschalot softens. Add the thyme leaves and cream, then simmer for 3 minutes until thickened slightly. Add the pasta and three-quarters of the cheddar to the sauce, stirring to coat.

Pile the mixture into the prepared baking dish, then scatter with the parmesan and remaining cheddar. Bake for 30 minutes or until bubbling and golden. Sprinkle with parsley, drizzle with a little extra truffle oil if desired, then serve with grilled bread.
* Truffle oil is available from gourmet food shops and delis.

PASTA

japanese prawn, pickled vegetable & noodle salad

Serves 4

1 cup (250ml) brown-rice vinegar* or regular rice vinegar
¼ firmly packed cup (50g) brown sugar
1 small carrot, cut into thin matchsticks
1 small cucumber, cut into thin matchsticks
250g soba or somen noodles*
2 spring onions, cut into thin matchsticks
¼ cup each coriander and mint leaves
1 long red chilli, thinly sliced
1 cup snow pea sprouts, trimmed
20 cooked prawns, peeled, deveined
2 tsp toasted sesame seeds

Dressing
1 tbs honey
¼ cup (60ml) tamari* or soy sauce
¼ cup (60ml) brown-rice vinegar* or regular rice vinegar
¼ cup (60ml) olive oil
2 tsp sesame oil

Place vinegar and sugar in a small pan and stir over low heat until sugar dissolves. Increase heat to medium-high and simmer for 10 minutes or until syrupy, then allow to cool. Add the carrot and cucumber and set aside to pickle for up to 1 hour – the longer you leave them, the better they are.

Cook the noodles according to packet instructions, then drain. Place in a large bowl with the drained pickled vegetables, spring onion, herbs, chilli, snow pea sprouts and prawns.

For the dressing, whisk all ingredients together in a bowl. Add to salad and toss to combine. Sprinkle with sesame, then serve.
* Available from Asian and health food shops.

sushi rice bowl

Serves 4

2 cups (440g) brown rice
Grated zest and juice of 1 orange and 1 lemon
2 tbs caster sugar
2 tbs Japanese shoyu* or regular soy sauce
2 tbs brown-rice vinegar* or regular rice vinegar
400g firm tofu, patted dry, cut into 2cm cubes
1 tbs sunflower oil
4 sheets nori seaweed*
4 spring onions, sliced on the diagonal
1 small Lebanese cucumber, sliced into long, thin strips
1 avocado, sliced into thin wedges
50g snow pea sprouts, ends trimmed
Black sesame seeds*, toasted white sesame seeds
   and pickled ginger (gari)*, to serve

Cook the rice in boiling salted water according to packet
instructions. Drain and allow to cool.

   Meanwhile, place the citrus zest and juice in a saucepan
with the sugar over medium-high heat. Stir to dissolve the sugar,
then boil for 1 minute. Remove from the heat and stir in the
shoyu and vinegar. Stir half the dressing into the cooled rice.

   Heat a chargrill pan or frypan over medium heat. Brush
the tofu with the oil and cook for about 1 minute, turning,
until golden on all sides.

   Line 4 serving bowls with the nori. Divide the rice among
serving bowls, then top with the spring onion, cucumber,
avocado and snow pea sprouts. Drizzle with the remaining
dressing then sprinkle with sesame seeds and ginger.
Serve with the chargrilled tofu.

* From Asian food shops and selected supermarkets.

chilli rice with barbecued duck

Serves 4

1 cup (200g) jasmine rice (or use 3 cups leftover cooked rice)
1 tbs sunflower oil
1 large red onion, thinly sliced
2 eggplants, cut into 2cm cubes
4 tbs chilli jam*
200g baby spinach leaves
1 Chinese barbecued duck*, meat removed, chopped
1/2 cup mint leaves
1/2 cup coriander leaves
Sliced long red chilli, to garnish

Cook the rice according to packet instructions. Cool.

Meanwhile, heat the oil in a wok over medium-high heat. Add the onion and stir-fry for 5 minutes or until starting to brown. Add the eggplant and cook, stirring, for 2-3 minutes until the eggplant starts to soften and turn golden.

Add the rice to the eggplant with the chilli jam, spinach leaves and duck meat and cook, stirring, for a further minute or until heated through. Remove from the heat, stir through the mint and coriander, then serve garnished with chilli.
* Chilli jam is available from selected supermarkets and delis. Duck is from Asian barbecue shops.

chicken paella

Serves 4-6

Olive oil
1 onion, finely chopped
2 chorizo sausages, peeled, sliced
3 streaky bacon rashers, rind removed, sliced into batons
2 cups (400g) calasparra* or arborio rice
1 tbs sundried tomato paste
280g jar chargrilled capsicum strips*, drained
3 tomatoes, seeds removed, chopped
3 garlic cloves, crushed
2 tsp smoked paprika* (pimenton)
1/4 tsp saffron threads
1.5L (6 cups) chicken stock
3/4 cup (185ml) dry white wine
1 barbecued chicken, cut into portions
1 tbs chopped flat-leaf parsley

Heat the olive oil in a large, deep frypan over medium heat. Add the onion, chorizo and bacon and cook, stirring, for 5-6 minutes until onion is soft and bacon is starting to crisp. Add the rice, stirring to coat in the mixture. Add the tomato paste, capsicum, tomato, garlic and paprika, then cook, stirring, for 2-3 minutes. Add saffron, chicken stock and wine, then bring to the boil. Simmer gently uncovered, stirring occasionally, for 15 minutes or until the liquid is evaporated and the rice is just cooked.

Meanwhile, cut the chicken meat into bite-sized chunks. Stir into the paella and cook for a further 2-3 minutes until heated through. Season to taste, then stir through parsley and serve.
* Chargrilled capsicum is available from supermarkets (see Glossary). Calasparra rice and smoked paprika are available from delis and gourmet food shops.

chicken & eggplant laksa

Serves 4

Chargrilled eggplant gives this laksa a wonderful smoky flavour.

4 slices chargrilled eggplant*, drained, cut into strips
250g thick rice-stick noodles
3-4 tbs laksa paste
400ml can coconut milk
600ml chicken stock
4 small chicken breast fillets, thinly sliced
1 lemongrass stem (pale part only), bruised
2 kaffir lime leaves*
150g sugar snap peas, halved lengthways or shredded
1 tsp brown sugar
Zest and juice of 1 lime
Thai basil* and coriander leaves, to serve

Pat the eggplant with paper towel to remove excess oil.
   Soak noodles in boiling water according to packet instructions until soft. Drain, then rinse in cold water and set aside.
   Heat a wok over medium heat and stir-fry the laksa paste for 1 minute or until fragrant. Stir in the coconut milk and stock, then bring to a simmer. Add the chicken, lemongrass and lime leaves and simmer for 6-8 minutes or until chicken is cooked through. Add the peas and eggplant and simmer for 2 minutes or until peas are just cooked. Stir in the sugar, zest and juice.
   Divide the noodles among bowls and top with the laksa. Garnish with Thai basil and coriander, then serve.
* Chargrilled eggplant is from delis and supermarkets. Kaffir lime leaves and Thai basil are from greengrocers and Asian food shops.

chocolate torte

Serves 6-8

A version of this clever torte by Australian cook Di Holuigue
appeared in *Vogue Entertaining + Travel* in the '80s and I've been
making it ever since. I love the idea that you use the same mixture
for the base and the filling – so simple yet sure to impress.

200g dark chocolate, chopped
200g unsalted butter, softened, chopped
½ cup (110g) caster sugar
6 eggs, separated
1 heaped tbs dry breadcrumbs
1 tbs unsweetened cocoa powder

Preheat the oven to 190°C. Line the base and sides of
a 22cm springform cake pan.

Melt the chocolate in a heatproof bowl over a saucepan
of simmering water (don't let the bowl touch the water).
Stir until smooth, then set aside to cool.

Place the butter and sugar in the bowl of an electric mixer
and beat until light and fluffy. Add the egg yolks, one at a time,
beating after each addition, then stir in the melted chocolate.

In a separate clean bowl, beat the eggwhites until stiff peaks
form. Fold one-third into the chocolate mixture to lighten, then
gently fold in the remaining eggwhite. Place two-thirds of the
mixture into a piping bag with a star nozzle and chill.

Add the breadcrumbs to the remaining mixture and spread
in the prepared pan. Bake for 20-25 minutes until firm.
Transfer to a rack to cool completely in the pan.

Turn out the cake and place on a serving platter. Bring the
topping mixture to room temperature. Starting in the centre,
pipe the topping over the cake in a spiral to completely cover.
Dust with cocoa powder, then slice and serve.

no-bake chocolate tarts

Serves 6

200g shortbread or digestive biscuits
100g unsalted butter, chopped
1 tbs golden syrup
100g milk chocolate, chopped
100g dark chocolate, chopped, plus extra melted
  chocolate to drizzle and shaved chocolate to garnish
1 tsp vanilla extract
2 tbs pure icing sugar, sifted
200ml thickened cream, plus extra to serve
Unsweetened cocoa powder, to garnish
Strawberries, halved, to garnish

Place the biscuits in a food processor and pulse to form fine crumbs. Place the butter and golden syrup in a saucepan over low heat, stirring, until butter melts, then pour into processor and pulse to combine. Press the biscuit mixture into the base and sides of six 10cm loose-bottomed tart pans. Chill until required.

Melt the milk and dark chocolate together in a heatproof bowl over a saucepan of simmering water (don't let the bowl touch the water). Remove from heat, stir until smooth, then allow to cool for 5 minutes. Stir in the vanilla and fold in the icing sugar.

Whip cream until soft peaks form, then fold into the chocolate mixture. Pour into the tart pans and chill for at least 2 hours until the chocolate filling is set.

To serve, drizzle plates with melted chocolate, top tarts with extra whipped cream and sprinkle with shaved chocolate and cocoa powder. Serve with strawberries.

refrigerator cake

Serves 8-10

Serve this cake as a dessert or in thin slices with coffee.
Keep in the fridge for up to 1 week.

150g pitted prunes, roughly chopped
1/3 cup (80ml) Pedro Ximénez sherry*, plus extra to serve
250g digestive biscuits, roughly chopped
100g raw pecans, chopped
100g unsalted pistachios, chopped
15 (about 50g) glacé cherries
150g unsalted butter, chopped
5 tbs golden syrup
500g dark chocolate, chopped
Cocoa powder, to dust

Line a 25cm x 10cm loaf pan with plastic wrap, leaving some
overhanging the sides to cover.
   Place the prunes and sherry in a small bowl and leave to
soak for 2-3 hours.
   Combine the biscuits, nuts and cherries in a bowl. Place the
butter, golden syrup and chocolate into a heatproof bowl over
a saucepan of simmering water (don't let the bowl touch the
water), stirring gently, until the chocolate melts. Remove from
the heat. Add biscuit mixture, prunes and any soaking liquid,
stirring to combine. Press mixture down well into the loaf pan to
expel any air bubbles, cover with the overhanging plastic wrap
and chill for at least 4 hours, preferably overnight, until set.
   Invert onto a platter and dust with cocoa just before serving.
Cut into 2cm-thick slices and serve with small glasses of sherry.
* Pedro Ximénez is a sweet, sticky Spanish sherry, available
from selected bottle shops.

blender chocolate mousse

Serves 4

Who doesn't love chocolate mousse? In this version, you simply throw everything in the blender so it's quick and easy.

1 cup (100g) finely chopped dark chocolate,
   plus extra grated chocolate to serve
¼ cup (55g) caster sugar
1 tsp instant coffee granules
2 tbs brandy
3 eggwhites
¾ cup (105ml) thickened cream,
   plus extra whipped to serve (optional)

Place the finely chopped chocolate in a blender.
   Place the sugar, coffee, brandy and ¾ cup (180ml) water in a saucepan over medium-low heat and bring to the boil, stirring to dissolve the sugar and coffee.
   With the blender motor running, carefully pour the hot liquid through the feed tube, blending until the chocolate has melted. Add the eggwhites and cream and pulse the blender several times to just combine.
   Pour the mousse into 4 serving glasses and chill for 4 hours or overnight. Serve topped with extra grated chocolate and whipped cream, if desired.

chocolate truffles

Makes 30

300ml thickened cream
1 tbs instant coffee granules
450g dark chocolate, chopped
¼ cup (60ml) Baileys Irish Cream or brandy
1 tsp vanilla extract
1 cup (100g) unsweetened cocoa powder

Combine the cream and coffee in a saucepan over medium heat, stirring, until coffee dissolves. Decrease heat to low and add the chocolate, stirring for 5-6 minutes until the chocolate melts. Set aside for 5 minutes to cool, then stir in the Baileys or brandy and vanilla. Pour into a shallow bowl, allow to cool, then chill for 4 hours until set to a fudge-like consistency.

Use a small ice-cream scoop to scoop balls from the chocolate mixture (or scoop out teaspoonfuls of the mixture and roll into balls wearing gloves). Place on a baking paper-lined tray in the fridge as you go – you should have enough mixture for 30 truffles.

Sift the cocoa onto a large sheet of baking paper. Roll the truffles in the cocoa to coat, then store the truffles in an airtight container or in the fridge for up to 5 days.

Bring to room temperature before serving, then dust with a little extra cocoa if needed.

rosewater cupcakes

Makes 12

These cakes are inspired by New York's famous Magnolia Bakery –
be generous with the icing, as that's what makes them so special.

180g unsalted butter, softened
350g caster sugar
4 eggs
1 cup (250ml) milk
1 tsp each vanilla extract and rosewater*
1½ cups (200g) self-raising flour
1 cup (150g) plain flour

Icing
500g unsalted butter, softened
350g pure icing sugar, sifted
Rose pink food colouring

Preheat the oven to 100°C and line a 12-hole muffin pan
with paper cases.

Place the butter in the bowl of an electric mixer and beat for
5 minutes until very pale. Gradually add the sugar and continue
to beat for a further 5 minutes until very light and pale. Add the
eggs, one at a time, beating well after each addition.

Combine the milk, vanilla and rosewater in a bowl. Sift the
flours and gently fold into the egg mixture using a metal spoon,
alternating with the milk mixture, until combined. Spoon into
paper cases, filling to just over halfway. Bake for 20 minutes
or until a skewer inserted in the centre comes out clean and
the cakes are lightly golden. Stand in the pan for 5 minutes,
then turn out onto a wire rack to cool completely.

For the icing, beat the butter, sugar and a few drops of
colouring with electric beaters until light and fluffy. Use a
piping bag with a fluted nozzle to ice the cakes generously.
* From supermarkets and Middle Eastern food shops.

easy baklava

Serves 6

500g unsalted mixed nuts (such as
   walnuts, pistachios and almonds)
250g honey
250g caster sugar
Zest and juice of 2 oranges
2 cardamom pods, smashed
1 cinnamon quill
16 sheets filo pastry
80g unsalted butter, melted
Ice cream, to serve

Preheat the oven to 200ºC. Spread nuts on a baking tray
and toast for 5 minutes. Cool slightly, then finely chop in
a food processor and set aside.

   Meanwhile, combine the honey, sugar, orange zest and juice,
cardamom, cinnamon and 300ml water in a pan over medium
heat. Boil for 5 minutes or until syrupy, then allow to cool.

   Lay 1 sheet of filo pastry on a bench and brush with butter.
Cover with another filo sheet and brush with more butter.
Sprinkle all over with a layer of nuts, leaving a 1cm border.
Fold in the 2 shorter ends and roll quite tightly into a log.
Place seam-side down on a greased baking tray, then repeat
with the remaining pastry, butter and nuts to make 6 rolls.
Bake for 5-6 minutes or until golden brown.

   Cool the rolls slightly, then cut into pieces. Place in a shallow
dish, pour over the cooled syrup, then stand for at least 1 hour.

   Serve with ice cream, drizzled with some of the syrup.

party lamingtons

Makes 18

I used to make huge platters of lamingtons for my two sons'
birthday parties. They're grown men now, but they still love them.

85g packet strawberry jelly crystals
85g packet orange jelly crystals
1 tbs unsalted butter
1 tbs cocoa powder
1/2 cup (80g) pure icing sugar, sifted
Twin-pack (350g) square vanilla sponge cake*
3 cups (270g) desiccated coconut

Boil 2 cups (500ml) water in the kettle. Place jelly crystals in
separate jugs. Pour 1 cup of boiling water over each and use
a fork to whisk until the crystals dissolve. Pour into separate
shallow dishes and chill for 1-1½ hours until just starting to set.
   Meanwhile, place the butter, cocoa powder, icing sugar
and 3 tablespoons boiling water into a shallow bowl. Stir
with a fork until coating consistency.
   Cut each cake into 9 squares. Spread the coconut on
a large plate or a sheet of baking paper.
   Dip 6 of the cake squares first in strawberry jelly, then
in coconut. Place on a rack to firm slightly. Repeat with
the remaining cake, dipping 6 in orange jelly and 6 in the
chocolate mixture, then coconut. (If the chocolate mixture
begins to set, stir in 1 tablespoon boiling water.)
* Available from supermarkets.

black forest cake

Serves 6

When I got married, it was the height of fashion to have a Black Forest cake at your wedding. Times have changed, but they're still a great cake for entertaining, especially when you start with a ready-made chocolate cake.

680g jar pitted morello cherries, drained, juice reserved
2 tbs sugar
1/3 cup (80ml) kirsch* or brandy
2 tsp arrowroot
2 tbs pure icing sugar, sifted
300g mascarpone cheese
350g store-bought chocolate slab cake or chocolate brownies
2 tbs cherry jam
1 tbs finely grated dark chocolate, to garnish
Zest of 1 orange, to garnish

Place the cherry juice in a saucepan over low heat with the sugar and half the kirsch or brandy. Mix the arrowroot with a little cold water until smooth, then add to the pan. Heat gently, stirring, for 2-3 minutes until thickened. Add the cherries to the sauce, then remove from the heat and set aside to cool.

Beat the icing sugar and mascarpone together in a bowl with a wooden spoon until combined.

Cut the cake into 6 pieces and place on a platter. Sprinkle over remaining kirsch and spread with the jam. Pile the mascarpone mixture on top of the cake pieces followed by some cherries and sauce. Sprinkle with chocolate and zest, then serve with remaining cherry sauce.

* Kirsch is a clear, unsweetened cherry brandy, from bottle shops.

chocolate mayonnaise cake

Serves 6-8

This is the perfect recipe for when you feel like baking a cake but discover you have no eggs! Who would've thought mayonnaise could turn into such a delicious dessert.

1²/₃ cups (250g) self-raising flour
60g cocoa powder
¼ tsp baking powder
200g caster sugar
¾ cup (225g) whole-egg mayonnaise
3 tsp vanilla extract
100g unsalted butter, softened
100g cream cheese
1²/₃ cups (250g) pure icing sugar, sifted
1 shot (30ml) Kahlua (or other coffee liqueur)
Hazelnuts half-dipped in melted chocolate, to decorate

Preheat the oven to 180°C. Grease and line the base of a 23cm springform cake pan.

   Place the flour, cocoa, baking powder, caster sugar, mayonnaise and 2 teaspoons of the vanilla in the bowl of an electric mixer with 200ml warm water and beat for 2-3 minutes until smooth. Spread into the prepared pan and bake for 40 minutes or until a skewer inserted in the centre comes out clean. Cool completely.

   Meanwhile, make the icing. Process the butter, cream cheese, icing sugar, remaining 1 teaspoon of vanilla and Kahlua in a food processor until smooth. Spread over the cooled cake and decorate with nuts.

berries with white chocolate sauce & sweet pangrattato

Serves 4

Italians use pangrattato, crisp fried breadcrumbs mixed with garlic or herbs, as a topping for pasta and other savoury dishes. This sweet version is flavoured with cocoa and cinnamon, and is great sprinkled over berry desserts.

450g mixed fresh berries (we used raspberries, blueberries and chopped strawberries)
2 slices sourdough, crusts removed, torn into pieces
$1/3$ cup (40g) almond meal
1 tbs brown sugar
1 tbs cocoa powder
1 tsp ground cinnamon
20g unsalted butter
$1/3$ cup (80ml) pure (thin) cream
250g white chocolate, chopped

Preheat the oven to 180ºC and line a baking tray with baking paper. Place the berries in the freezer to chill while you make the pangrattato and sauce.

Place the bread in a food processor with the almond meal, sugar, cocoa and cinnamon. Process the mixture to form fine crumbs, then add the butter and pulse to combine. Spread on the prepared tray and bake for 10 minutes or until crisp and dry. Remove from the oven and allow to cool.

Meanwhile, place the cream and chocolate in a heatproof bowl over a pan of simmering water (don't let the bowl touch the water) until chocolate melts, then stir gently to combine.

Divide the berries among plates, pour over the warm sauce, then serve sprinkled with the sweet pangrattato.

no-pastry pear tarts
Makes 6

If you don't have time to make your own poached pears, use fresh
pear or buy ready-made poached pears from gourmet food shops.

180g unsalted butter
50g plain flour
180g pure icing sugar
100g almond meal
2 tsp fincly grated lemon zest
5 eggwhites
2 poached pears*, sliced (or 2 fresh pears, thinly sliced)
2 tbs flaked almonds
Icing sugar, to dust
Pure (thin) cream or ice cream, to serve

Preheat the oven to 200°C. Lightly grease six 7cm
loose-bottomed tart pans.
   Melt the butter in a small saucepan over medium heat for
1-2 minutes (watch closely and don't let it burn), until golden
brown. Allow to cool.
   Sift the flour and icing sugar into a bowl and stir in the
almond meal, lemon zest and melted butter.
   Use a fork to lightly froth the eggwhites in a separate bowl,
then fold into the dry ingredients. Divide among the tart pans
and place pear on top. Scatter with flaked almonds and bake
for 10 minutes. Reduce the heat to 170°C and bake for a further
5-6 minutes or until golden. Dust with icing sugar and serve
warm with cream or ice cream.
* Poached pears are from gourmet food shops (see Glossary).

little fig & rosewater pies

Makes 4

450g packet frozen sour cream shortcrust pastry*
  (or use a 375g block frozen puff pastry), thawed
4 fresh figs
4 sugar cubes
2 tsp rosewater*
1 egg, beaten
Icing sugar, to dust
Thin (pure) cream, to serve

Preheat the oven to 200ºC. Line a baking tray with paper.

Roll out the pastry on a lightly floured surface to 5mm thick. Cut four 10cm and four 12cm circles from the pastry.

Trim the stalk from each fig, then turn over. Cut a cross in the base, then squash down a little with your hand to flatten and open out slightly. Press a sugar cube into the cross of each fig and sprinkle with the rosewater.

Sit each fig right-way up in the centre of the larger pastry rounds and brush the border with beaten egg. Cover with the smaller pastry rounds, then fold in the edges of the larger pieces and pinch the edges to seal. Place on the lined tray. (You can keep the tarts chilled at this stage for 3-4 hours until ready to bake.)

Just before baking, brush the pies all over with beaten egg, then cook in the oven for 25 minutes or until the pastry is golden and the fig juices are starting to ooze.

Dust the warm pies with icing sugar and serve with cream.
* Sour cream pastry is available from delis and gourmet food shops (see Glossary). Rosewater is available from Middle Eastern and gourmet food shops.

apple galette

Serves 4-6

The secret to this wonderfully crisp galette is to bake it with another tray on top so the pastry doesn't have a chance to rise but remains crisp, thin and buttery.

6 Granny Smith apples
2 tbs lemon juice
375g block frozen puff pastry, thawed
100g unsalted butter, chopped
185g caster sugar
Cream or ice cream, to serve

Preheat the oven to 180°C. Line a baking tray or pizza tray with baking paper.

Peel and core the apples, then slice very thinly (a mandoline slicer is ideal). Gently toss with the lemon juice to prevent the slices from discolouring.

On a lightly floured surface, roll out the pastry to 5mm thick and trim into a neat 28cm-diameter circle. Place on the lined tray. Arrange the apple slices in overlapping circles – with each slice overlapping to ensure that they all fit on the base. Dot with the butter and sprinkle with half the sugar. Cover with another sheet of baking paper and second heavy baking tray. Bake for 35 minutes.

Gently remove the top tray and baking paper (being careful of the hot juices). Sprinkle with the remaining sugar, then return to the oven, uncovered, for a further 10-15 minutes until well caramelised. Slice the galette and serve warm with cream or ice cream.

simple summer pudding

Serves 6

When my husband, Phil, and I lived in England, working as a
butler and cook team, we made this pudding every weekend
for weddings and parties. Then we had the stress of unmoulding
them, but this simple version is made in a dish for easy serving.
For me, it's the quintessential English dessert.

600g frozen mixed berries
1/2 cup (110g) caster sugar
10 slices white bread, crusts removed,
   halved into triangles
Pure (thin) cream, to serve

Place the fruit in a saucepan with the sugar and 1/4 cup (60ml)
water and bring to the boil over medium heat. Reduce the heat
to low and simmer for 3-4 minutes until the sugar dissolves
and the fruit starts to give off some of its juice.

Layer one-third of the bread in a 1-litre (4-cup) serving
dish, cutting pieces to fit if necessary. Using a slotted spoon,
top the bread with half the berry mixture. Repeat with another
layer of bread and fruit, then finish with the final layer of
bread. Pour the liquid remaining in the pan over the bread,
pressing down well. Cover and chill for at least 30 minutes,
then serve drizzled with cream.

caramel
pavlova bites

Makes 15 bites

When you make a pavlova, you always end up with leftover egg yolks, so I like to use them up in an easy caramel filling that's made in the microwave. With their crisp meringue shell, creamy caramel and tart raspberries, these little bites are quite addictive!

2 eggwhites
1 cup (220g) caster sugar
1 tsp white vinegar
1 tsp vanilla extract
1 heaped tbs cornflour
Thick cream, fresh raspberries and icing sugar, to serve

Microwave caramel
2 egg yolks
20g unsalted butter
1/2 cup (125ml) milk
1/2 firmly packed cup (100g) brown sugar
1 tbs plain flour
1 tsp vanilla extract

Preheat oven to 120°C. Line 2 baking sheets with baking paper.
  Beat eggwhites using electric beaters until soft peaks form. Gradually add sugar, beating until stiff and glossy. Gently fold in vinegar, vanilla and cornflour. Using a piping bag fitted with a 1cm nozzle, pipe a 5cm circle onto the tray, then continue to pipe 3-4 rings on top of each other around the rim to form a nest. Repeat to make 15 meringues. Bake for 30 minutes, then leave meringues in switched-off oven to cool completely (at least 2 hours).
  For the filling, whisk ingredients together in a microwave-safe bowl. Microwave on medium setting for 3 minutes, stirring every minute, until thickened. Beat well to remove any lumps, then cool.
  Spoon caramel into the cooled pavlova nests, then top with cream and raspberries. Dust with icing sugar just before serving.

bread & butter pudding

Serves 4-6

Bread and butter pudding must be one of the easiest desserts to make, and a universal favourite. The secret to a creamy texture is to let it stand for at least 1 hour before baking.

⅓ cup (55g) sultanas
2 tbs brandy
10 slices white bread, crusts removed
50g unsalted butter, softened
5 eggs
300ml pure (thin) cream
300ml milk
¼ cup (55g) caster sugar
1 tsp vanilla extract
Icing sugar, to dust
Thick cream or ice cream, to serve

Grease a 1-litre (4-cup) baking dish. Place the sultanas and brandy in a small pan and warm through over low heat for 3-4 minutes. Set aside.

Lightly butter the bread, then cut the bread into 2 triangles. Layer the bread in the baking dish, overlapping slightly, scattering with sultanas and any remaining brandy as you go.

Lightly whisk the eggs, cream, milk, sugar and vanilla until combined. Pour the mixture evenly over the bread and leave to soak for 1 hour.

Preheat the oven to 180°C.

Place the baking dish in a roasting pan and pour in enough boiling water to come halfway up the sides of the dish. Bake for 40 minutes or until the top is golden but the custard still has a slight wobble. Stand for 10 minutes, then dust with icing sugar and serve with cream or ice cream.

cheesecake in a glass

Serves 4

200g shortbread biscuits
1/3 cup (80ml) dessert wine or sweet sherry
2 gold-strength gelatine leaves*
Zest and juice of 1 lemon
250g cream cheese
500g thick Greek-style yoghurt
1/2 cup (110g) caster sugar
Berry compote or warmed berry jam, to serve

Place the shortbread in a food processor and pulse to form crumbs. Place crumbs and wine in a bowl, then stir to combine. Divide among four 1-cup (250ml) serving glasses. Set aside.
    Soak the gelatine in cold water for 5 minutes to soften.
    Meanwhile, heat the lemon juice in a microwave for 30 seconds. Squeeze excess water from the gelatine, then add the leaves to the hot lemon juice and stir to dissolve.
    Place the cream cheese, yoghurt, sugar, lemon zest and gelatine mixture in a food processor and process until smooth. Pour over the biscuit mixture and chill for at least 2 hours or until set. Top with the berry compote and serve.
* Gelatine leaves are from gourmet food shops. Always check the packet for setting instructions.

limoncello soufflé

Makes 8

Melted butter, to brush
¹/₄ cup (55g) caster sugar, plus extra to dust
6 eggwhites
Pinch of cream of tartar
325g jar good-quality lemon curd*
Grated zest of 1 lemon
2 tbs limoncello*, plus extra chilled to serve
Icing sugar, to dust

Preheat the oven to 200°C. Brush eight 150ml soufflé dishes
or ramekins with melted butter. Dust with a little extra caster
sugar, tapping to remove excess.

   Use electric beaters to whisk the eggwhites and cream of
tartar until soft peaks form. Gradually add the sugar, beating
constantly, until the mixture is stiff and glossy.

   Meanwhile, gently warm the curd and zest in a saucepan
over low heat. Stir in the limoncello, then transfer to a large
bowl. Use a large metal spoon to gently fold one-third of
the eggwhites into the lemon mixture. Continue to fold in
the remaining eggwhite until just combined, taking care not
to lose too much volume. Divide among ramekins and run
your finger around the inside edge of each ramekin. Bake for
12 minutes or until golden and risen. Dust with icing sugar,
then serve immediately with extra chilled limoncello.
* Good-quality lemon curd is from gourmet food shops and delis
(see Glossary). Limoncello is an Italian-style lemon liqueur,
available from bottle shops.

rosé wine jellies

Makes 6 individual or 1 large jelly

6 gold-strength gelatine leaves*
3/4 cup (165g) caster sugar
2 cups (500ml) rosé wine
Pure (thin) cream and summer fruits (optional), to serve

Lightly grease six 150ml dariole moulds or one 900ml jelly mould. Soak gelatine in cold water for 5 minutes to soften.

Place the sugar in a pan with 200ml water and stir over low heat until the sugar is dissolved. Remove from the heat.

Squeeze excess water from gelatine and add the leaves to the warm sugar mixture, stirring to dissolve. Stir in the wine, then divide among moulds. Allow to cool, then chill for at least 4 hours until set.

Turn the jellies out onto serving plates and pour over a little cream. Serve with summer fruits such as raspberries and peaches, if desired.

* Gelatine leaves are from gourmet food shops. Always check the packet for setting instructions.

blanco y negro

Serves 6

Leche merengada is a lovely Spanish ice cream that's just so refreshing as it doesn't contain egg yolks. Topped with espresso, it becomes blanco y negro, the Spanish version of Italy's affogato.

2 cups (500ml) full-cream milk
150ml thickened cream
150g caster sugar
Grated zest of 1 lemon
2 cinnamon quills
1 tbs brandy
3 eggwhites
Hot espresso coffee, to serve
Almond praline (optional), to serve

Place the milk, cream and 100g of the sugar in a saucepan over medium heat with lemon zest and cinnamon quills. Bring to just below boiling point, then remove from the heat and stand for 40 minutes to infuse. Strain through a sieve into a large bowl, discarding solids, then stir in the brandy.

In a separate bowl, use electric beaters to whisk the eggwhites and remaining 50g sugar until stiff peaks form. Gently fold into the milk mixture.

Pour the mixture into a shallow container and freeze for 2-3 hours until frozen at the edges. Remove from freezer and beat with electric beaters, then refreeze. Repeat this process two or three times. (Alternatively, churn in an ice cream machine following manufacturer's directions.)

When ready to serve, place a large scoop of ice cream in four serving glasses. Pour a shot of espresso coffee over each one and serve with praline if desired.

pistachio & date kulfi

Serves 6

These make-ahead desserts are the ideal cooling
finish to an Indian feast.

$^2/_3$ cup (100g) unsalted pistachio kernels
395g can sweetened condensed milk
300ml thickened cream
125g fresh pitted dates, chopped
1 tbs orange blossom water*
3 oranges
$^1/_2$ cup (110g) caster sugar

Line six 150ml dariole moulds with plastic wrap, leaving
some overhanging the sides.
  Process pistachios and condensed milk in a food processor
until nuts are finely chopped and you have a coarse paste.
  Lightly whip the cream in a large bowl, then fold in the
condensed milk mixture, dates and orange blossom water.
  Divide the mixture among the dariole moulds, then cover
with the overhanging plastic wrap and freeze for at least
6 hours or overnight until firm.
  Zest the rind of 1 orange using a zester. Place in a saucepan
with the juice of 2 oranges, the caster sugar and $^1/_2$ cup (125ml)
water. Stir over low heat to dissolve the sugar, then simmer for
5 minutes until the syrup has thickened. Set aside to cool.
  When ready to serve, peel the remaining orange, then slice
the flesh into rounds. Place on a serving plate and drizzle with
some of the candied rind and syrup. Turn out the kulfi onto
plates, then drizzle with the remaining rind and syrup and
serve with the orange slices.
* Fresh dates are from greengrocers. Orange blossom water
is available from supermarkets.

frozen ricotta & mascarpone puddings

Makes 6

These creamy little parcels are the perfect accompaniment to hot Christmas pudding or fruit mince pies.

1 cup (240g) fresh ricotta
1 cup (250g) mascarpone cheese
1 cup good-quality fruit mince*
1/3 cup (80ml) Grand Marnier or Cointreau
3 tbs thick cream
1 tbs icing sugar

Cut twelve 23cm squares of muslin. Lightly beat the ricotta, mascarpone, fruit mince and liqueur with electric beaters until combined. Stir in the cream and icing sugar.

   Layer 2 muslin squares on top of each other and spoon about 1/2 cup of the mixture into the centre. Enclose in the fabric and shape into a ball, then tie with kitchen string. Repeat with remaining fabric and mixture. Freeze for 6 hours or overnight until firm. Serve with hot Christmas pudding or fruit mince pies.
* Good-quality fruit mince is from gourmet food shops.

profiteroles with ice cream and chocolate sauce

Serves 6

A yummy warm chocolate sauce and vanilla ice cream give the old-fashioned profiterole a new lease on life.

300ml good-quality vanilla ice cream
30 store bought profiteroles*, split
250g good-quality dark chocolate, roughly chopped
1/2 cup (125ml) thickened cream
Splash of Cognac or brandy

Allow the ice cream to soften in the fridge for 30 minutes. Sandwich each profiterole with a scoop of softened ice cream, then return to the freezer on a tray as you go. This can be done up to a week in advance.

When almost ready to serve, place the chocolate, cream and alcohol in a saucepan over low heat until the chocolate has melted. Stir gently to combine, then serve the warm sauce drizzled over the profiteroles.

* From Italian grocers and selected supermarkets.

ice cream pie

Serves 6-8

400g chocolate cream biscuits (such as Oreos)
120g unsalted butter, melted
150ml dry white wine
2 tbs brandy
Finely grated zest and juice of 2 lemons
Finely grated zest of 1 orange
1 tsp vanilla extract
1/3 cup (70g) caster sugar
500ml thickened cream
2 mangoes

Line the base of a 22cm loose-bottomed tart pan with baking paper.

Pulse the biscuits to fine crumbs in a food processor. Add the melted butter and pulse briefly to combine. Press the crumb mixture well into the base and sides of the tart pan. Chill while you make the filling.

Clean the food processor, then add the wine, brandy, citrus zest and juice, vanilla and sugar. Process to combine and dissolve the sugar, then add the cream with the motor running and process for about 1 minute until the mixture is thick and well combined. Pour the mixture into the tart shell and freeze for at least 3 hours until firm. Transfer the tart to the fridge about 30 minutes before serving to soften slightly.

Meanwhile, clean the food processor again and blend the mango flesh to a smooth puree.

When ready to serve, remove the tart from the pan and place on a platter. Drizzle with some of the puree, then slice and serve with the remaining sauce on the side.

Apple and sage jelly (p 113)
Tracklements Apple & Sage Jelly from Simon Johnson,
1800 655 522, simonjohnson.com.au.

Bouquet garni (p 58)
Herbie's Spices, (02) 9555 6035, herbies.com.au.

Chargrilled capsicum (p 29, 139, 194)
Sacla Char-Grilled Capsicums from supermarkets.

Chermoula paste (p 144)
Greg Malouf, gregmalouf.com.au; or
Christine Manfield, christinemanfield.com.

Chilli chocolate (p 73)
Lindt Chilli Chocolate from supermarkets.

Frozen French-style crepes (p 12)
Creative Gourmet French Style Crépes from
supermarkets.

Harissa (p 185)
Christine Manfield, christinemanfield.com.

Herbes de Provence (p 40)
Herbie's Spices, (02) 9555 6035, herbies.com.au.

Lemon curd (p 236)
Duchy Originals Organic Traditional Lemon Curd from
Simon Johnson, 1800 655 522, simonjohnson.com.au.

Peperonata (p 151)
Sacla Peperonata from supermarkets; or Woolworths
Select Peperonata from Woolworths supermarkets.

Peri peri spice mix (p 147)
Herbie's Spices, (02) 9555 6035, herbies.com.au.

Pikelet bites (p 32)
Golden Pikelet Bites from supermarkets.

Poached pears (p 223)
Simon Johnson Pears In Red Wine from Simon Johnson,
1800 655 522, simonjohnson.com.au.

Pomegranate molasses (p 78)
Mymouné Pomegranate Molasses from Simon Johnson,
1800 655 522, simonjohnson.com.au.

Porcini powder (p 77)
The Essential Ingredient, (02) 9557 2388,
essentialingredient.com.au.

Roasted cherry tomatoes in oil (p 51)
Sacla Sweet Cherry Tomatoes from supermarkets.

Sage and onion stuffing mix (p 119)
Tandaco Stuffing Mix Sage & Onion from supermarkets.

Sour cream shortcrust pastry (p 224)
Carême Sour Cream Shortcrust Pastry. For stockists,
visit caremepastry.com.

ACKNOWLEDGEMENTS

Firstly, a sincere thanks to the management team at News Magazines – particularly Sandra Hook and Wendy Miller for giving me this opportunity. Also to Brigitta Doyle and Liz White at ABC Books, for their invaluable input on this project.

To the editorial team on *delicious.*, I have to mention you all by name as I feel privileged to work with such a talented and dedicated group of people. Thank you to editor-in-chief Trudi Jenkins for all your encouragement and support over the past seven years. And to editor Kylie Walker, who joined us at a particularly crazy time but has thrown herself into the madness with such energy.

To deputy editor Danielle Oppermann (my rock), I couldn't have done this without your eye on the details and disciplined approach to making it all come together... just in time. To the subediting team of Sarah Macdonald, Molly Furzer, Selma Nadarajah and Amira Georgy, and editorial coordinator Alison Pickel – thanks for your all your efforts and your patience, particularly on those occasions when I was up to my elbows in food and couldn't come to the phone.

A thousand thanks to our senior designer Simon Martin, whose enthusiastic input into the book has helped to make it such a visual delight, and designer Liz Bucknell, again a new recruit, who has helped keep the magazine looking beautiful while we were somewhat distracted.

A special hug must go to my wonderful food team. To Olivia Andrews, my assistant food editor – although she was eating her way around China while we were shooting the book, she was no less involved – your support and hard work keep the magazine looking so great every month. And to Georgina Kaveney, who along with Youjin Kwon did such a great job in assisting on the book shoot and making it all run so smoothly.

Lastly, a heartfelt thanks to the amazing team on the book shoot. Photographer Brett Stevens, your talent has turned my basic vision into such beautiful images. Stylist David Morgan – I am such a fan, thank you for making every dish look so special. And last but not least, to our creative director Scott Cassidy, whose lack of cooking skill is certainly made up for by creative talent – thank you for going on this journey with me and taking the book to a level I could only have dreamed of.

THANKS TO THE FOLLOWING STOCKISTS

Design Mode International Mona Vale (02) 9998 8200; **Ici et Là** Surry Hills (02) 9699 4266, icietla.com.au; **Kris Coad** Stockists (03) 9690 6510, kriscoad.com; **Meïzai** stockists nationally 1800 674 455, meizai.com.au; **Mud Australia** Stockists nationally (02) 9519 2520, mudaustralia.com; **No Chintz** Willoughby (02) 9958 0257, Woollahra (02) 9386 4800, nochintz.com; **Parterre** Surry Hills (02) 9356 4747, Woollahra (02) 9363 5874, Fortitude Valley (07) 3666 0100, parterre.com.au; **The Bay Tree** Woollahra (02) 9328 1101, thebaytree.com.au.

Published by HarperCollins Publishers Ltd

Originally published in Australia in 2008 by ABC Books for
the Australian Broadcasting Corporation and reprinted by HarperCollins*Publishers* Pty Limited.

First Canadian edition

HarperCollins books may be purchased for educational, business, or sales
promotional use through our Special Markets Department.

HarperCollins Publishers Ltd
2 Bloor Street East, 20th Floor
Toronto, Ontario, Canada
M4W 1A8

www.harpercollins.ca

Library and Archives Canada Cataloguing in Publication
information is available upon request

ISBN: 978-1-44343-169-9

Food Director Valli Little
Photography Brett Stevens (Ian Wallace p 151, 202, 212, 224)
Styling David Morgan (Louise Pickford p 151, 202, 212, 224)
Creative Director Scott Cassidy
Senior Designer Simon Martin
Project Editors Molly Furzer, Sarah Macdonald, Danielle Oppermann
Food preparation Georgina Kaveney, Youjin Kwon
delicious. **Editor-in-chief** Trudy Jenkins
delicious. **Editor** Kylie Walker
International Business Director, News Magazines: Wendy Miller
Chief Executive Officer, News Magazines Sandra Hook

Printed and bound in Canada
9 8 7 6 5 4 3 2 1